IS LITERARY HISTORY
POSSIBLE?

IS LITERARY HISTORY
POSSIBLE?

David Perkins

THE JOHNS HOPKINS UNIVERSITY PRESS

Baltimore and London

© 1992 by The Johns Hopkins University Press
All rights reserved
Printed in the United States of America

The Johns Hopkins University Press
701 West 40th Street
Baltimore, Maryland 21211-2190
The Johns Hopkins Press Ltd., London

∞ The paper used in this book meets the minimum requirements of
American National Standard for Information Sciences — Permanence of
Paper for Printed Library Materials, ANSI Z39.48–1984.

Library of Congress Cataloging-in-Publication Data

Perkins, David, 1928–
Is literary history possible? / David Perkins.
p.   cm.
Includes bibliographical references and index.
ISBN 0-8018-4274-3 (alk. paper)
1. Literature — History and criticism — Theory, etc. I. Title.
PN441.P36   1992
809'.001 — dc20   91-22516

for Jens Rieckmann

CONTENTS

PREFACE

THIS IS A BOOK ON THE THEORY OF LITERARY HIS-
tory. It deals with fundamental problems that arise in the
writing of it. The aspects it concentrates on are two: the
aporias of form or, in simpler terms, the insurmountable
contradictions in organizing, structuring, and presenting
the subject; and the always unsuccessful attempt of every
literary history to explain the development of literature
that it describes. My procedure is empirical. I have not
tried to theorize answers to the dilemmas I discuss. If I
hoped to be thorough and fair, there was hardly space to
point them out. Moreover, except on minor points, I
think no answers can be suggested.

The book analyzes the assumptions and practices of
particular literary histories in order to test the plausibility of their versions of the past. I have drawn on examples
of literary history from the beginnings of the discipline
in the eighteenth century, but most of my instances are
very recent, since current thought and practice is the primary concern. The history of literary history is a fascinat-
ing one — one that has not hitherto been narrated except
in pieces. I have kept it in mind and frequently com-
mented on it, but it is a subject for another book, and the
effort to write it would encounter all the problems I
explore in this one.

Portions of chapter 5 appeared in *Nineteenth-Century
Literature* and of chapters 2 and 3 in *New Literary His-*

tory. They are used here with the kind permission of the editors of the journals. Much of chapter 4 and a few paragraphs of chapter 1 were included in *Theoretical Issues in Literary History* (1991), which I edited, and they are reprinted with the permission of the Harvard University Press. I am grateful to audiences at the University of Denver, the California Institute of Technology, the University of California at Los Angeles, the University of Washington in Seattle, and the Poetry Colloquium of Harvard University for very helpful discussions, and I am no less indebted to the students in my seminars on this subject at Harvard.

Translations are my own unless the notes indicate otherwise. I have used the traditional *he* when the gender is indefinite.

IS LITERARY HISTORY
POSSIBLE?

1

The Present State of the Discussion

CONCEPTS AND EXAMPLES OF LITERARY HISTORY
can be found in the works of critics from Aristotle on. Yet
the discipline of literary history, as it was practiced in the
nineteenth century, could not narrate its own history
without locating an origin. Hence, it was and is usually
said that literary history began in antiquarian works of
the eighteenth century. Assimilating ideas of Herder and
the Schlegels, the discipline became intellectually profound. Its major modes have been Hegelian, naturalist,
positivist, *geistesgeschichtlich*, Marxist, formalist, sociological and, paradoxically, postmodern. In variants, the
theories of Darwin, Spengler, Wölfflin, Weber, Adorno,
Foucault, Bloom, Geertz, and many others have been
pressed into service. The genre includes works on the literature of nations, periods, traditions, schools, regions,
social classes, political movements, ethnic groups, wom-
en, and gays, and these studies may foreground the genesis or production of texts, their effect on society or on
subsequent literature, their reception, or all these moments synthetically.

For approximately the first seventy-five years of the
nineteenth century, literary history enjoyed popularity
and unquestioned prestige. It was characterized, at this
time, by three fundamental assumptions: that literary
works are formed by their historical context; that change
in literature takes place developmentally; and that this

1

change is the unfolding of an idea, principle, or suprapersonal entity. Viewing literary works in relation to their historical context, we can, it was argued, achieve a juster interpretation and a more complete appreciation than is otherwise possible. We can explain features of texts as products and expressions of the social structures, ways of life, beliefs, literary institutions, and so on, of the communities in which they were created. As a synthesis of history and criticism, literary history seemed more powerful, for some purposes, than either discipline separately.

The premise of a developmental history is that an event goes "through a series of changes," as Dilthey puts it, "of which each is possible only on the basis of the previous one."[1] Transition of this kind has continuity. The next phase preserves much of the former. There are no jumps, reversals, returns, clean slates, or beginnings. Developmental history explains a work by what it immediately evolves from. The contexts in which it places a work exist simultaneously with or just prior to the work. The view of developmental history is limited in this respect, since literary works may be directly modeled on ones produced centuries earlier in alien societies.

All of the most important literary histories in the nineteenth century were narratives, and they traced the phases or sometimes the birth and/or death of a suprapersonal entity. This entity might be a genre, such as poetry; the "spirit" of an age, such as classicism or romanticism;[2] or the character or "mind" of a race, region, people, or nation as reflected in its literature. Despite their large differences on other points, all schools of literary history shared this way of conceiving their subject. It was common to the comparative literary history of Friedrich and August Wilhelm Schlegel, to literary histories influenced

---

[1] Wilhelm Dilthey, *Der Aufbau der geschichtlichen Welt in den Geisteswissenschaften* (Frankfurt a. M.: Suhrkamp, 1970) 201.

[2] For example, H. A. Korff, *Geist der Goethezeit* (Leipzig: Koehler and Amelang, 1923–57).

by Hegel and by his supplementer and critic in the philosophy of history, Wilhelm Dilthey, to the naturalistic approach of Taine, and to the great, popular histories, such as those of Scherer, Brandes, and De Sanctis. What is still the most widely read of all literary histories, Nietzsche's *The Birth of Tragedy*, was, for its time, idiosyncratic in its uses of speculative psychology, but it sought to disclose the mind of the ancient Greeks. The alternative would be a literary history that attributed less unity to its subject. Extreme examples are the "postmodern" *Columbia Literary History of the United States* (1987) and the *New History of French Literature* (1989), both of which are a collection of separate essays and deliberately avoid consecutiveness and coherence.

These suprapersonal entities were analogous, in some ways, to what Dilthey, with reference to historiography in general, calls "ideal unities" or "logical subjects," such as nations, religions, and classes. These exist through individuals but extend beyond them and, "by the content, value, purpose that realizes itself in them, possess an independent existence and their own development. Thus they are subjects of an ideal sort. A certain knowledge of reality is in them; purposes are realized in them; in the interconnected realm of the spiritual world they have a significance and assert it" (162–64). Historians predicated concerning them as though they were individuals, asserting that they rose, battled, flourished, exerted influence, and so forth,[3] and Paul Ricoeur justifies this practice, though with qualifications, by comparing such logical subjects to characters in a novel: "The role of character can be held by *whomever* or *whatever* is designated in the narrative as the grammatical subject of an action predicate in the basic narrative sentence 'X does R.'"[4]

---

[3] Such sentences may rest on very different views of the ontological status of logical subjects. For discussion, see Arthur C. Danto, *Narration and Knowledge* (New York: Columbia UP, 1985) 258–61.

[4] Paul Ricoeur, *Time and Narrative,* trans. Kathleen McLaughlin

Most literary historians now conceive such terms as *Restoration drama, gothic novel,* and *Imagist movement* as generalizations or as designations of types, rather than as names of principles, ideas, or ideal beings, but such terms are still essential to the discipline. They express a "synthesis of works" by different writers, in Roland Barthes's phrase,[5] and, unless one perceives such syntheses, one cannot write literary history. The assumption that the various genres, periods, schools, traditions, movements, communicative systems, discourses, and epistemes are not baseless and arbitrary groupings, that such classifications can have objective and valid grounds in the literature of the past, is still the fundamental assumption of the discipline, the premise that empowers it.[6] Whether literary histories are justified in this assumption, whether either their particular classifications of literary works or the processes by which they classify can be adequately defended, are questions to which I return in chapter 4.

The advantages of nineteenth-century literary histories were manifold and enormous. The premise that the history of literature exhibits the development of "the national conscience," as Croce put it,[7] provided a sense of purpose and wide social significance for the work. So also with other entities or subjects. Brandes's *Main Currents in Nineteenth Century Literature* is not a national but a comparative literary history, analyzing the "psychology of the first half of the nineteenth century" in several coun-

and David Pellauer (Chicago: U of Chicago P, 1984) 1:197. Ricoeur argues the point at length.

[5] Roland Barthes, *Critical Essays,* trans. Richard Howard (Evanston: Northwestern UP, 1972) 161.

[6] Peter Szondi, *Hölderlin-Studien: Mit einem Traktat über philologische Erkenntnis* (Frankfurt a. M.: Insel, 1967) 20–21, perceives this and uses it as a reason for rejecting literary history as it has usually been practiced.

[7] Benedetto Croce, Introduction to Francesco de Sanctis, *History of Italian Literature,* trans. Joan Redfern (New York: Harcourt, Brace, 1931) 1:vi.

tries.[8] It was just as important to know the mind of the age, or of the preceding period that had formed your own, as the mind of your nation in its long historical development. With the unfolding of an idea, principle, suprapersonal entity, or *Geist* as its subject, a literary history became teleological. It acquired a plot, could assume a point of view, and might generate considerable narrative interest.

This conception of literary history provided relatively clear criteria of selection and emphasis. One knew what texts to include: whichever contributed to the plot, to the development of the *Geist*. Thus one did not have to answer, or, at least, one confronted much less anxiously than literary historians now do, fundamental questions about the definition and scope of literature. Is literature, for the purposes of literary history, only the "best" writings, or does it also include popular works that are judged qualitatively inferior? Should literary histories focus only on the moments of innovation and high achievement, or should they distribute their space as time was spread out in the past, when "whole centuries" were devoted to "imitation and mere development"?

Raising the issue at the start of his 1812 *Lectures on the History of Literature,* Friedrich Schlegel resolved to give only "cursory notice" to the long, barren tracts.[9] However we answer such questions, they are fraught with the most far-reaching consequences for a representation of literary history and for its ideological impact and cultural politics. Swayed by the aesthetic criteria of their time and place, both Charles Richardson and Barrett Wendell decided that there was virtually no literature worth mentioning in America for the first two hundred years of settlement. In contrast to later historians of American lit-

[8] Georg Brandes, *Main Currents in Nineteenth Century Literature* (New York: Macmillan, 1906) 1:vii.

[9] Friedrich Schlegel, *Lectures on the History of Literature* (London: George Bell, 1896) 22.

erature, they devoted nine-tenths of their pages to the nineteenth century.[10]

Or—to raise another question—does literature mean only works in certain genres—poems, dramas, novels—or does the literary historian also exhibit, and not as background only, discourses in philosophy, theology, politics, science, medicine, and so on? Through most of the nineteenth century the answer was obvious. The "field of literature" must be extended, as Louis Cazamian said, to comprehend "philosophy, theology, and the wider results of the sciences."[11] In 1917, the editors of the *Cambridge History of American Literature* still conceived of their subject as "the life of the American people as expressed in their writings rather than a history of *belles lettres* alone."[12]

The "psychology of the . . . nineteenth century," the "story of the English mind,"[13] the "life of the American people"—pursuing such subjects, literary historians interested themselves almost exclusively in the contents of works, in the emotions and thoughts they express, the ideals and moral values of their authors, and the social manners and institutions, material and economic life they reflect. Thus, in twenty-three pages on Anglo-Saxon poetry, J. J. Jusserand, in *A Literary History of the English People*, has, typically, one page on a point related to form or artistry—namely, versification—and otherwise concentrates on the reflection in this poetry of the joy of the Anglo-Saxons in battle, their elegiac sorrow, their sense

[10] Charles F. Richardson, *American Literature (1607–1885)* (New York: Putnam's, c. 1886–88); Barrett Wendell, *A Literary History of America* (New York: Scribner's, 1900).

[11] Emile Legouis and Louis Cazamian, *A History of English Literature*, 2d ed., rev. (New York: Macmillan, 1930) 2:xiii.

[12] *Cambridge History of American Literature*, ed. William P. Trent et al. (New York: Macmillan, 1917–18) 1:iii.

[13] Henry Morley, quoted in René Wellek and Austin Warren, *Theory of Literature* (New York: Harcourt, Brace, 1942) 263.

of fate and of the finality of death; in short, on the "manners and beliefs of the northern peoples."[14]

No wonder, then, that this once flourishing discipline came under attack. Its conception of literature was clearly inadequate and reductive. From its beginning, literary history had been accompanied by strenuous probing of grounds and debating of methods. But for a long time this theorizing was only a struggle of different schools of literary history. Gradually, however, the worth of the whole discipline was questioned. The assault is clearly visible at the end of the nineteenth century in critics touched by fin de siècle aestheticism, such as Edmond Scherer and Emile Faguet. They point out that historical contextualism can explain everything except what, perhaps, one most wants to explain—"genius"; in other words, the qualitative difference between works of art produced in exactly the same time and place.[15] Historical contextualism can interpret and account for elements of texts by referring them to relevant bits of the social and literary matrix, but it cannot grasp texts as aesthetic designs. This argument has often been forgotten and never answered, and I revive it at more length in chapter 6.

Others made the complaint, also still valid, that because literary history emphasizes the social, collective determinants of texts and their reception, it wallows in the minor, drearily reviewing insignificant authors. This polemic continues to the present day. In it, literary history is usually identified only, and quite unjustifiably, with positivist literary history, which is, its critics say, a history of just about everything except literature. It

[14] J. J. Jusserand, *A Literary History of the English People* (1895), 3d. ed. (London: T. Fisher Unwin, 1925) 42.

[15] Edmond Scherer, *Essays on English Literature* (New York: Scribner's, 1891) 76; Emile Faguet, *Politiques et moralistes du dix-neuvième siècle*, 3d. ser. (Paris: Lecéne, Oudin, n.d.) 268. These critics are cited merely as representative. The argument was made repeatedly and by many persons.

presents names, titles, groups, movements, influences, and external information of all kinds—biographical, political, social, *geistesgeschichtlich*—but, as Roland Barthes says in attacking Gustave Lanson, "the work *escapes*," for the work is "*something else* than its history, the sum of its sources, influences, or models."[16]

The theories of the Russian Formalists, set forth between 1916 and 1928, were a stage in this argument. The Formalists, who are discussed in chapter 7, did not question the value or the possibility of writing literary history but denied that literary changes could be explained by events external to literature. Instead, they traced laws and mechanisms of development that are immanent within it. At about the same time as the Formalists, Croce mounted his powerful attack on literary history. The essence of Croce's position was that, since every work of art is unique, it cannot be reduced to the classification and generalization that are necessary in writing a literary history. For Croce, the uniqueness of a text is the locus of its value, its art; hence, literary history, which is useful for certain practical purposes, perforce exhibits the less important aspects of the texts it considers.

In the United States, the New Criticism programmatically rejected literary history. Reacting to abuses of *Geistesgeschichte* during the Nazi period, scholars in Germany taught and practiced a similarly "immanent" mode of reading after the Second World War. Deconstructive criticism exposed the logical aporias involved in periods, genres, and other classifications hitherto essential to literary history[17] and, deploying arguments different from the Aesthetes, Croce and the New Critics undermined the confidence of the discipline. Objects as self-contradictory,

[16] Roland Barthes, *On Racine*, trans. Richard Howard (New York: Octagon, 1977) 154–55.

[17] Paul de Man, "Literary History and Literary Modernity," in *Blindness and Insight*, 2d. ed., rev. (Minneapolis: U of Minnesota P, 1983); Jacques Derrida, "The Law of Genre," in *On Narrative*, ed. W. J. T. Mitchell (Chicago: U of Chicago P, 1981).

indeterminate, and uninterpretable as are texts in deconstructive readings are not easily subject to generalizations.

Now, however, a generation of scholars is returning to literary history. I have in mind sociological literary histories, studies of the institution of literature in past ages and of the "literary field," histories of reception, analyses of the diachronic modification of genres, many New Historicist essays, much *Ideologiekritik*, and constructions of the literary traditions of women, gays, ethnic groups, political movements, socioeconomic classes, and new, third world countries. The authors of these works are reconsidering the theory of literary history and providing new models of what it should be, and thus they are responding anew to the imperative, voiced at the very start of modern literary history by the Schlegel brothers, that history and theory should be one.[18]

The revival of literary history can be explained as an inevitable reaction to its long suppression. This would be an internal or immanent explanation, since it locates the cause of change not in outward events but within the university study of literature as a quasi-autonomous institution. It posits that a law of change operates, so that whatever discourse—for example, the New Criticism—is long dominant must be replaced by a discourse with different and probably opposite assumptions. The mechanisms that cause such changes might be found in the pressures for visibility in university careers, in the need of graduate students to produce new theses on texts that have already been much discussed, and in other material factors. But we may also note that any dominant discourse loses interest as it becomes more familiar, if only because it disappoints the promise it once seemed to hold and reveals its intellectual limitations.

Usually, however, the reviving interest in literary history is explained by external, contextual considerations.

[18] August Wilhelm Schlegel, *Vorlesungen über Aesthetik I (1798–1803)*, ed. Ernst Behler (Paderborn: Ferdinand Schöningh, 1989) 181.

Students of the 1960s are now professors and have not completely lost the political motivations of their youth. They stress the interrelations between social formations and literature because society remains a prime object of their concern. As *Ideologiekritik*, their scholarship foregrounds the ideological aspects of texts from the past for the purpose of intervening in the social struggles of the present. To deny the involution of social conflicts and power relations in literary and critical texts would leave our profession politically irrelevant. (The counterargument is that with respect to political struggles the academic study of literature is inherently sheltered and retreative. Professors feel guilty about this and expose political and ideological determinants of texts in order to quiet conscience.)[19]

The movements for liberation of women, blacks, and gays produce literary histories for the same motives, essentially, that inspired the national and regional literary histories of the nineteenth century. These groups turn to the past in search of identity, tradition, and self-understanding. Their histories do not usually stress discontinuity but the opposite. They find their own situation reflected in the past and partly explained by it, not (in their opinion) because they are projecting their situation on the past, but because the same situation of suppression or marginalization continues from the past into the present. To see it this way is part of their protest.[20]

The new literary histories are shaped out of many

[19] See the sharp phrasing of Alan Liu in "The Power of Formalism: The New Historicism," *English Literary History* 56 (Winter 1989): 751: "In the mirror of desire named the 'Renaissance' the interpreter can *fantasize* about subverting dominance while dreaming away the total commitments of contestation."

[20] But see Dominick LaCapra, *History & Criticism* (Ithaca: Cornell UP, 1985) 133, on "the vicious paradox by which a certain class of scholars establish their own disciplinary hegemony through a vicarious appeal to the oppressed of the past."

intellectual sources: hermeneutic philosophy, Russian Formalism, cultural anthropology, sociology, communications theory, and cultural semiotics. Reconsideration of Marxist premises has afforded more nuanced and penetrating conceptions of literature (and literary histories) as ideological and of the dialectical development of literature. Foucault encouraged his readers to reject the traditional, romantic model of literary change as continuous development and to emphasize, instead, the discontinuity and contingency of history. Under his inspiration, literary texts were resituated by relating them to discourses and representations that were not literary. Foucault was often classified as a structuralist, but he disowned the label. If we take him at his word, French structuralism contributed little directly to the revival of literary history.

Structuralist ways of thinking were basic to important reconceptions of literary history in essays by Yury Tynyanov and by Czech Structuralists, such as Jan Mukařovský and Felix Vodicka, but French structuralists did not build on these writings. Nevertheless, structuralist thought had a significant impact on other types of history and on debates about historiography, and these models and debates are also certain to eventually have their impact on literary history. One thinks of the exchanges between Sartre and Lévi-Strauss and between the *Annales* school and its opponents. Hayden White's analyses of the rhetorical determinants of historical representations will also become important for literary historians, and I am much indebted to White for my own analyses in chapter 2.

Thus literary history is again at the turbulent center of literary studies. This book participates in the revitalized theorizing about it, but it is skeptical. I have followed the reconstruction of the discipline with the keenest interest and sympathy, and yet, having tried to write literary history, I am unconvinced (or *de*convinced) that it can be done. There is nothing unusual about this change of mind. In fact, there are distinguished precedents among literary historians—Benedetto Croce, R. S. Crane, and René Wellek.[21] I raise again, with reference to both the new and the traditional conceptions of the genre, the very old question, is it possible to write literary history?[22]

The question is whether the discipline can be intellectually respectable. Hundreds of books and articles testify every year that literary history can be written.[23] But can the project fulfill its own intention? To address this question, we must obviously know the aim of literary history, and this is not a point to be settled lightly. To judge from what literary histories actually do, the aims are many: to recall the literature of the past, including much that is now seldom read; to organize the past by selecting which authors and texts are to be discussed and by arranging them into interconnected groups and narrative sequences; to interpret literary works and account for their character and development by relating them to their historical contexts; to describe the styles and *Weltanschauungen* of texts, authors, ages, and so on; to express the contents of works and quote passages from them, since many readers will have no other experience of these works; to bring, through selection, interpretation, and evaluation, the lit-

[21] See R. S. Crane's splendid, very skeptical book, *Critical and Historical Principles of Literary History* (Chicago: U of Chicago P, 1971), and René Wellek's "The Fall of Literary History," in *The Attack on Literature and Other Essays* (Chapel Hill: U of North Carolina P, 1982).

[22] René Wellek begins his chapter on "Literary History" in *Theory of Literature* 263: "Is it *possible* to write literary history, that is, to write that which will be both literary and a history?" Compare Uwe Japp, *Beziehungssinn: Ein Konzept der Literaturgeschichte* (Frankfurt a. M.: Europäische Verlagsanstalt, 1980) 219: "The question whether literary history is at all possible as a strict scholarly discipline."

[23] Japp, *Beziehungssinn* 32: "One must bear in mind that from the standpoint of a theory every literary history that has been written can be criticized and refuted. Nevertheless, as one must wonderingly confirm, there are literary histories. . . . Few disciplines have, apparently, so little to do with each other as the writing of literary history and the theory of literary history."

erary past to bear on the present, with consequences for both the literature and the society of the future. Some of these overlapping aims are obviously possible, even if others may not be.

Whatever else they have also hoped to accomplish, all literary historians have sought to represent the past and to explain it. To represent it is to tell how it was and to explain it is to state why—why literary works acquired the character they have and why the literary series evolved as it did. To take these—representation and explanation—as the general aims of the discipline and, therefore, as criteria for evaluating the success of literary histories, is not, it should be stressed, to impose personal, external, or unfair standards but ones that have been accepted within the discipline for almost two hundred years. Of course representation and explanation can never be complete, as literary historians and theorists have always recognized. Even if a historian knew all the relevant facts and answers, he could not crowd them into a book. The only complete literary history would be the past itself, but this would not be a history, because it would not be interpretive and explanatory.

The question is how much incompleteness is acceptable. Incomplete representations and partial explanations are not usually criticized as seriously distorting the past by their omissions. But if a literary historian leaves out particular considerations that are important to other historians, or if his account of the past is obviously not thick enough, incompleteness will be viewed as misrepresentation. Just where the frontier of acceptability lies is always disputable.

I come now to the crucial question of objectivity. And what could this ideal mean in practice, since it is self-evident that a literary history must be written from a point of view? The point of view, moreover, cannot be that of someone in the past, though this may be included. It must be determined by the personality, interests, and values of the historian. Anyone who examines the voluminous writings on the two most famous cruxes of literary history, the Shakespeare question (did Shakespeare or someone else write the plays?) and the Homer question (was there a Homer?), will find that after evidence is marshaled, the answers are also influenced by personal criteria, especially by moral and social assumptions. Some of the anti-Stratfordians resent authority and the scholarly establishment; others believe that a commoner of limited education and social rank could not have written such plays. John Keble was one of several Victorian critics who thought that to dissolve Homer into a collection of anonymous bards was morally debilitating. Such a conclusion seemed to question the power of an individual to transcend his age through qualities of mind and character.[24] Keble's argument itself illustrates that the point of view of a literary historian is formed by the world in which he lives. Our image of the past must change as the present does. "As flowers turn their heads to the sun," says Walter Benjamin, "the past turns to the sun that is rising in the heaven of history."[25] So much has always been clear to literary historians. At the moment, theorists are virtually unanimous in regarding literary histories as, at best, merely hypothetical representations. They are provisional statements in our ongoing dialogue with the past and with each other about the past. Or they are heuristic constructions and help us to see some things more clearly by obscuring others.

And yet, most literary historians also imply, tacitly, that the past had a being, a reality, was so and not otherwise. In a given time and place, a work was read in a certain way by certain persons, and—this is the assumption—reception history can partly recover their experience. In the process of its genesis, a work was deter-

[24] John Keble, *Lectures on Poetry, 1832–41*, trans. Edward Kershaw Francis (Oxford: Clarendon, 1912) 1:99.

[25] Walter Benjamin, "Über den Begriff der Geschichte," in *Gesammelte Schriften*, ed. R. Tiedemann and H. Schweppenhäuser (Frankfurt a. M.: Suhrkamp, 1972) 1:694–95.

mined more by certain factors and less by others. The factors cannot be fully known, but they are not completely inaccessible.

Typically, then, literary historians believe they can advance knowledge even though they take for granted that their reading of the past can only be partial and provisional. In each written history of it, the past is different, and yet one cannot say anything one likes about a past event. "The sources," as Reinhart Koselleck puts it, "have the power of veto. They forbid us to venture or admit interpretations that can be shown on the basis of the sources to be false or unreliable."[26] Since historians assume that the past existed objectively, each new version of the past, so long as it is a plausible version, can be viewed as a gain. Each history leaves a deposit of accurate information and reasonable interpretation to be synthesized by the next, along with the deposits of other previous histories. According to Ricoeur, "the credo of objectivity is nothing other than [the] twofold conviction that the facts related by different histories can be linked together, and that the results of these histories can complete one another" (176).

Such is the faith of positivist historiography, which reminds us that our image of the past changes not only because it reflects a changing present, but also because we constantly know more about the past. I think the assumption that the past had a determinate being is very questionable, but I do not explore the issue here, since it is a philosophic one for another book. My point is only that the assumption is implied in the sorts of effort that go into the writing of literary histories and in the criteria by which they are reviewed. If we did not make this assumption, knowledge of the past could be said to change but not to increase, and the latest literary history of the United States, the *Columbia Literary History of the United States* (1987), would not be more reliable than the

[26] Reinhart Koselleck, *Futures Past: On the Semantics of Historical Time*, trans. Keith Tribe (Cambridge: MIT P, 1985) 155.

first one in 1829. Disputes among literary historians could not be resolved by the procedures of the discipline, that is, by research and inference, and the settling of disputes would merely illustrate the sociobiology of academic life. The value of literary histories might be informative, aesthetic, humanistic, or political. In other words, they might present a selection of information about the past, appeal to our sense of form and our imagination, satisfy our hunger for wisdom, or fortify our political commitments and our ideologies, but they would not be knowledge.

Though the past is finally inaccessible, we can reasonably require that interpretations of it be plausible. There would, of course, be no point even in this requirement unless we assumed that a partial knowledge of the past is more likely to be revealing than distorting, an assumption we make, but for which we have no adequate ground. The criteria of plausibility include the rules of historiography as a discipline: pertinent information must be sought and weighed, statements must cohere logically, judgments must be backed up and cannot rest on the mere ipse dixit of the historian, sources must be criticized, and so on. The criteria also include whatever assumptions concerning human character and motivation, the probable causes of events, and the structure of reality are now accepted. Historical interpretations and explanations cannot themselves transcend the time and place in which they are produced.

If plausible explanation is our aim, as I think it must be, we must recognize that this implies a social consensus. What is plausible in one community will not be in another. A historical explanation that posits a spirit—or Geist—is credible only if one believes in such spiritual beings. In most universities in the Western world, a student who explains historical events as the immediate will of God would be instructed to seek secondary, natural causes. Only these count within the discipline of history. And rightly so. Recognizing that the assumptions one lives by may ultimately be ideological and contingent, one should question and test them, but one cannot step outside of them at will. *Plausibility* must ultimately mean plausibility for me and for whoever thinks as I do. This view of the matter does not in the least imply blithe tolerance of whatever opinion someone happens to maintain. The effort for plausibility is strenuous and self-corrective, if only because the criteria of credibility one happens to hold necessitate this.

The question, then, of whether literary history is possible is really whether any construction of a literary past can meet our present criteria of plausibility. Finally, we cannot answer with a yes or no. A judgment of *more* or *less* is required, and many considerations must be weighed. The course of my argument tends, however, toward the negative. In the final chapter, I shift the question, inquiring not whether literary history is possible, but whether it is necessary. This move is modeled on a passage in Samuel Johnson that still seems crushing. Whether literature is desirable is, Johnson agrees, debatable, for whatever may be a source of happiness can also be a cause of misery. But, says Johnson, if the debate is referred "to *necessity*, the controversy is at an end."[27] So also with literary history. It has an indispensable role in our experience of literature and a broader social or cultural function as well. My opinion is, then, that we cannot write literary history with intellectual conviction, but we must read it. The irony and paradox of this argument are themselves typical of our present moment in history.[28]

[27] Samuel Johnson, "Reflections on the Present State of Literature," *Universal Visitor* (April 1756). Reprinted in "A Project for the Employment of Authors," *Works* (Oxford: Oxford UP, 1825) 5:356.

[28] See, for example, Ackbar Abbas, "Metaphor and History," in *Rewriting Literary History*, ed. Tak-Wai Wong and M. A. Abbas (Hong Kong, 1984), where Abbas works out the implications of Paul de Man's views on literary history. He finds that de Man gives literary history "the paradoxical status of being an ever-present impossibility" (177).

The chapters that follow omit several arguments that have already been much discussed by others: the criticism of literary history by Croce and the New Critics; the hermeneutic difficulties, among which the problem of semiotic play, foregrounded by deconstruction, is only one; the blindness or distortion induced by ideological investments; and the impossibility of verifying statements made by literary historians and of demonstrating causal connections between historical events, since these events are, by definition, unique and unrepeatable.

Also, I do not dwell on the one solid reason known to me for thinking that a literary history might be objective and impersonal. If a literary historian—or any good reader—is shown a text, he may be able to infer when it was composed, even though he has never read it before. The historical development of the language gives him clues, and so does the context. But even without these aids, he would know the provenance of the text from its style. This fact, which no one disputes, illustrates that period styles exist and that their characteristics are objective.[29] We recognize them; we do not invent them.

This book concentrates, then, on certain fundamental cruxes in the theory of literary history and, in doing so, tries to foreground relatively novel aspects. Chapters 2 and 3 take up the problem of major form in literary histories. "The relationship of representation," says Dilthey, assumes "that within certain limits what is given and what is discursively thought are exchangeable" (150–51). He here assumes, with meaningless qualification ("within certain limits"), what he ought to prove, namely, that rep-

---

Compare Siegfried J. Schmidt, "On Writing Histories of Literature: Some Remarks from a Constructivist Point of View," *Poetics* 14 (Aug. 1985). Schmidt's first subheading is "Writing histories of literature: A necessary and impossible project." Japp 27: the present is dominated by "*one* figure of argumentation, that first affirms that there is a crisis in history and literary history, in order to show again from the crisis the—renewed—necessity of literary history."

[29] Compare Crane 108.

resentation is possible. The question is whether the formal rules or procedures of written discourse, which literary history must obviously follow, do not necessitate that history cannot represent the past but must distort it.

The writing of literary history involves selection, generalization, organization, and a point of view. It selects for representation only some of the texts and relevant events in the tract of past time it supposedly describes; it collects these into general entities (e.g., romanticism); it adopts a point of view toward them; and it makes them constituents of a discursive form with a beginning, a middle, and an end, if it is Aristotelean narration, or with a statement, development, and conclusion, if it is an argument.[30] In itself, the past, we suppose, had a different being. Historians were well aware of this discrepancy in the eighteenth century, and history was then classified as a form of literature. In the nineteenth century, however, the prestige of the sciences necessitated that history be included among them. Accordingly, the extent to which historical representations are determined by necessities of rhetoric was largely forgotten.

Recently, however, our awareness of the omnipresence of rhetoric in discourse has been growing. Thirty years ago, literary studies and the social sciences were in separate compartments; in each, the work of the other was more or less ignored. Literary critics studied rhetoric and fictional representation, and historians (and even literary historians) made representations of the past without considering that these also were rhetorical in form and were even, in many cases, like literary fictions. Now, however, we increasingly see that the past is necessarily transformed in the effort to represent it discursively.

This book focuses on what is perhaps the most important and certainly the least-considered aspect of this large theme. This is the problem of major form, in other words, of the structure that organizes and interrelates the

[30] Japp 49–50, 66.

results of research and conveys them to the reader. I discuss two forms of literary history: encyclopedic and narrative. The latter is a traditional form of literary history; encyclopedic form is also traditional and is now reemerging as the preferred form of postmodern literary history. Both forms actually prevent a literary historian from presenting a sophisticated conception of past realities. Encyclopedic literary history deliberately forfeits coherence, and narrative cannot express its subject with the required complexity. It cannot exhibit the simultaneity of diverse durations, levels of reality, sequences of events, and multiple points of view. At least this is true of narrative within the discipline of history, which contrasts for necessary reasons with fictional narrative. Even more serious, perhaps, is that the form in which we write cannot greatly differ from the form in which we think. A narrative historian is committed not only in his book but also in his consciousness to conceptions of causality, continuity, coherence, and teleology in events, and he must suppress whatever perceptions do not fit with his plot construction.

Chapters 4 and 5 take up an even more fundamental move in writing literary histories. For a prior and still more basic organization of the field of objects must precede the major structuring of it. This is the arranging of texts and authors into groups. If this process has no plausibility, literary history must also lack it, and I analyze the process in general by considering a number of particular examples. The purpose is to see by what methods and on what grounds literary historians divide or combine authors and texts, positing suprapersonal entities such as periods, schools, movements, and genres. Chapter 5 traces the history of a particular suprapersonal entity, showing the steps, stages, reasons, motives, and ideological factors by which, over sixty years, it was constructed.

Chapters 2–5 deal with the organization of the literary past. But a literary history also attempts to explain the past; that is, it gives reasons why literary works have whatever characteristics they do and why literature developed as it did. These explanations may be either contextual or immanent; in other words, they explain either by events and conditions of the historical world that produced the text or by reference only to previous literature or literary institutions. In either case, they may expound laws of literary development, processes that supposedly operate universally. In chapters 6 and 7 I try, again analyzing particular examples, to test the adequacy of explanation in literary history, to assess whether either contextual or immanent answers, or a mixture of both, can be plausible.

One very important type of literary history is written for the purpose of distorting, attacking, or revising the past, or repressing a portion of it. Poets and novelists frequently generate such literary history in order to clear space for their own work. It is also produced by politically and ideologically committed persons for the sake of their cause. Such literary history observes Nietzsche's warning, in his second *Untimely Meditation*, that too much knowledge of history can undermine conviction and energy, and that in order for us to be able to live, the present must at times apply its strength to the destruction and dissolution of the past. The past must be critically attacked or "forgotten if it is not to become the grave-digger of the present."[31] If we are intent on forgetting or destroying the past, we are hardly striving to produce a seriously plausible version of it, and nothing that I discuss is problematic for literary histories of this type.

Also, I do not devote attention to the type of literary history advocated by Claus Uhlig in his 1982 *Theorie der Literarhistorie*.[32] The only literary history we can determine, says Uhlig, is that implicit in the work itself. For

---

[31] Friedrich Nietzsche, "Vom Nutzen und Nachteil der Historie," in *Werke in zwei Bänden* (Munich: Carl Hanser, 1967) 1:116.

[32] Claus Uhlig, *Theorie der Literarhistorie* (Heidelberg: Carl Winter, 1982).

example, in *Hamlet*, act 5, scene 7, Gertrude's description of Ophelia's drowning alludes to the dying swan motif; literary history makes this allusion visible by exhibiting previous and subsequent uses of the motif by different authors. Or, as another example, Milton's *Paradise Lost* acquired certain of its characteristics from its lateness in the history of the epic, a fact that Milton understood and comments on in the poem; literary history explores Milton's sense of this lateness as it is expressed in the text and as it affected his work. Hard pressed by the attacks on literary history, Uhlig thus reduces the discipline to unobjectionable acts of reading. In my opinion, Uhlig's retrenchment surrenders too much. He no longer asks questions that have made the discipline interesting and challenging.

Perhaps this is the place to notice the type of historically situated reading of single texts that Jerome McGann advocates. The question is whether such readings count as literary history. McGann would interpret the literary work within a historical context (or group of contexts) that is always highly particular. Reflecting on a methodology similar to McGann's, Karl Otto Conrady decides that the perspective on "a work in its . . . inextricable interwovenness with the specific social-historical object" is different from that of literary history, for the latter "seeks to discover lines leading backwards and forwards in time."[33]

My objection is different and may seem paradoxical. McGann's readings would elucidate "whatever in a poem is most concrete, local, and particular to it." "Everything about every poem that has ever been written" is "time- and place-specific."[34] From the point of view of literary

[33] Karl Otto Conrady, "Illusionen der Literaturgeschichte," in *Literatur und Sprache im historischen Prozess. Vorträge des Deutschen Germanistentages Aachen 1982*, ed. Thomas Cramer, vol. 1, *Literatur* (Tübingen: Max Niemeyer, 1983) 13.

[34] Jerome McGann, *The Beauty of Inflections: Literary Investigations in Historical Method and Theory* (Oxford: Oxford UP, 1985) 131, 202.

history, McGann insists too strongly on the particularity, the definitiveness of each moment of the past and of each poem. For the purposes of literary histories, these must be time- and place-characteristic. Only those aspects of literary works and their reception that are representative of a time and place can be the subject of a historical generalization and enter into literary history.[35]

Literary histories can focus on different moments of the total process. Usually they track literary change by noting the moment of origin, that is, they describe new works as they successively appear. Alternatively, however, they may concentrate on the moment of reception, when works are encountered by readers, or on the moment of impact, when works have their effects on other writers and on society. Ideally, a literary history would pursue all of these moments, but this ideal is visionary and cannot be realized in practice. In this book, I do not consider literary histories of reception and impact, primarily because the arguments would be different (though analogous); and to note distinctions among the different kinds of literary histories and to make frequent, partial exceptions for some of them would make the discussion longer without making it much more illuminating. However, I do not think that literary histories of reception and impact can overcome what is problematic in literary history as a discipline, and I shall try to say why.

The history of reception is now a vast, flourishing project of scholarship and theoretical debate. For the sake of brevity and focus, my questions refer mainly to the programmatic statement or manifesto of this field, H. R. Jauss's essay on "Literary History as a Challenge to Literary Theory." Jauss identifies literature with the immediate "experience of the literary work by its readers."[36]

---

[35] LaCapra (132) also criticizes overcontextualization, which he associates with "neo-positivist and antiquarian approaches." His point is that overcontextualization "excessively restricts the interaction between past and present."

[36] H. R. Jauss, "Literary History as a Challenge to Literary Theory,"

But of literature in this sense there cannot be a history. For the experience is too personal and inaccessible to be known by someone else or even completely by the person engaged in it, and even if this were not the case, the experience is not fully representable in language. Even in types of criticism, such as close readings, which attempt to describe such experiences, the most minute report is selective and abstract in relation to the actual event. And, of course, the reading differs on the next occasion and by another person on the same occasion. There is a contradiction between the collective and generalizing discourse of literary history and the individuality of literary response.

This argument applies also to other past events besides readings, since every battle, cabinet meeting, harvest, or voyage is also a unique happening and has dimensions unknown to the historian, especially with regard to the intimate, personal reactions of individuals. But in reading literature, such personal, intimate, even unconscious aspects of the experience are important. That the text moves and speaks to individuals at these levels is a main reason why it is read at all. If the history of literature were a history of responses to texts, it would have to be written with the knowledge that a large part of its subject is, in principle, inaccessible.

But this argument does not militate against literary history based on reception. Theorists of this discipline presuppose that no act of textual reception is identical with another.[37] The history of reception attempts to identify literary and sociological factors that condition but do not totally determine individual receptions in a given time and place. It seeks general, shared influences that for readers of a certain kind or members of a certain

in *Toward an Aesthetic of Reception,* trans. Timothy Bahti (Minneapolis: U of Minnesota P, 1982) 20.

[37] Ibid. 23. Compare H. F. Plett, *Textwissenschaft und Textanalyse, Semiotik, Linguistik, Rhetorik* (Heidelberg: 1975) 80, quoted in Gunter Grimm, *Rezeptionsgeschichte* (Munich: Wilhelm Fink, 1977) 16–17.

social group shape, up to a point, readings, interpretations, evaluations, and applications of a particular text. Because they are collective, these factors form a basis for literary history.

Jauss and many of his followers advance the concept of horizons of expectations and the blending (*Verschmelzung*) of these. The horizon of expectations is the nexus of readers' anticipations with respect to a given literary work. In any time and place, the horizon differs with, and is partly determined by, the work, but the horizons blend into those of successively higher orders. If these could be reconstructed, they would establish transpersonal bases for literary history, which would be a history of changing horizons of expectation from age to age. In a given time and place, the general horizon of expectations would account for the coherence of the literature produced and the relatively unified reception of past works.

Reception history is acutely vulnerable to the difficulties of structuring and grouping that I discuss in later chapters. The difference is that, instead of grouping authors and texts, the historian of reception would attempt to classify readers and their horizons. And instead of narrativizing the chronological succession of texts, he would narrativize the succession of horizons. But the literary history of reception would face a further structural complication. New texts are continually produced, but the same texts are received over and over through time. A reception history of English literature would feature Shakespeare in every period since 1600. This is a formal reason why narrative literary histories can more readily focus on the production of texts than on their impact or reception.

Moreover, there is the practical difficulty that, for most times and places, we lack the sources, such as accounts of reading experiences, from which a history of reception could be written. Conceding this, Jauss believes that we may also recover the horizon of expectations by studying the literary text itself, since the horizon for which it was written is implicit in the work. However, the attempt to deduce the horizon of expectations from the literary work is equally as personal, subjective, and time- and place-determined as any other act of literary interpretation. In other words, while we attempt to reconstruct a past horizon of expectations, we stand within our own. By Jauss's own hermeneutic principles, this mediation of the past horizon through our present one inevitably alters the past. This point is implicit in Jauss's argument, but is not foregrounded, since, from his perspective, it weakens the argument. Like most literary historians, he hopes to represent as closely as possible the past as it was.

Even if there were not this difficulty, I would still question the usefulness of the horizon of expectations as a concept. As I understand Jauss, he would include in the horizon primarily those expectations that are formed by reading literature. His position on this issue is complicated and compromising, however, and he gives different emphases in different contexts. For example, he speaks of expectations formed from a "pre-understanding of the genre, from the form and themes of already familiar works, and from the opposition between poetic and practical language" (22), and he is generally much impressed by the Russian Formalist principle that literary works are always seen against the background of previous literary works. On the other hand, he argues against the Russian Formalists that "the evolution of literature . . . is to be determined not only immanently through its own unique relationship of diachrony and synchrony, but also through its relationship to the general process of history" (18).

Presumably, then, he would also give prominence to readers' expectations that are created by economic, political, and cultural developments. For if literary historians reconstruct a horizon of expectations by considering only literature, there would be a wide gap between the responses to literature that the horizon would determine and those that actually existed.[38] As soon, however, as we admit the role of extraliterary events in shaping expectations, we introduce many more factors and make it less possible to reconstruct the horizon of expectations for a given work.

If Jauss (though not reception theory in general) pays far too little attention to the expectations formed by sociological circumstances—that is, by the race, gender, class, and so forth to which readers belong—the reason is instructive. If he paid attention to these sociological variables, he would confront too many different horizons of expectation, especially with the spread of literacy in the modern period. The more horizons we discriminate, the less they blend into one. Thus Jauss's theory tends to ground the coherence of a past age at the expense of its real heterogeneity. Every theorist of literary history—every practical attempt in the genre—ultimately shatters on this dilemma. We must perceive a past age as relatively unified if we are to write literary history; we must perceive it as highly diverse if what we write is to represent it plausibly.

[38] Robert Weimann seized on this point as a basis of his critique of Jauss in "'Rezeptionsästhetik' und die Krise der Literaturgeschichte," *Weimarer Beiträge* 8 (1973): 21–22. Weimann argues that Jauss's concept of the horizon of expectations divorces it from *Wirkungsgeschichte*, the history of the effects of literary works on society, and also from real history (*Realgeschichte*). "Neither the real life activity nor the ideology of the reader, nor even literary sociological reality are taken as the basis, but [rather] the reflex of subjective expectations contained in the literary work."

2

Narrative Literary History

THOUGH NARRATIVE HISTORY IS A WELL-RECOG-
nized form, we do not usually think of literary history as
narrative. Nevertheless, literary history may fulfill the
essential criteria of narrative, for it may and very often
does describe a transition through time from one state of
affairs to a different state of affairs, and a narrator reports
this transition to us. As the hero of a Horatio Alger novel
goes from rags to riches, the novel in several different
retellings of its origin and rise emerges from obscurity
and gradually flourishes, ascending like Pamela.

It is astonishing how readable and popular, yet informed and intelligent, narrative literary history can
sometimes be, and especially was in its great nineteenth-
century examples, such as Hippolyte Taine's *History of
English Literature* (1863), Francesco de Sanctis's *History
of Italian Literature* (1870–71), Georg Brandes's *Main
Currents in Nineteenth-Century Literature* (1872–90), or
George Saintsbury's *Short History of English Literature*
(1898). Brandes describes "a historical movement partak-
ing of the form and character of a drama. The six different literary groups it is my intention to represent may be
looked on as six acts of a great play."[1] His words indicate
how much he was imbued with the conviction that liter-

---

[1] Georg Brandes, *Main Currents in Nineteenth-Century Literature*
(New York: Macmillan, 1901) 1:ix.

ary history could have the structure and interest of a work of literature.

A high point of this nineteenth-century confidence in literary history as narrative is reached in Julian Schmidt's *History of German Literature since the Death of Lessing* (1866). Schmidt says in his preface:

> In the history of spiritual life it is not otherwise than in political history: in it also the reciprocal relation and impact of the heroes allows itself to be developed in the form of ground and consequence. At least I have felt it to be so as I strove to study in its inner connection the spiritual development from the first battles of healthy human understanding and feeling against the compulsion of the church up to our own day. It seemed to me that this spiritual battle of Germany formed a picture quite as unified and interconnected as any spiritual battle, in other words, that it qualified itself completely for the form of narrative.[2]

Schmidt's ringing words suggest several things about narrative literary history. Like all traditional narrative, it presents an entity—or hero—going through a transition. In a literary history, the hero cannot be a person but only a social individual or ideal subject; here it is the spirit of Enlightenment. A moment in its existence is taken as the beginning (the first battles) and a subsequent one as the terminal point (today). In the second moment, the inner or outer state of the hero is not the same as it was at first, and the middle of the narrative accounts for this change; in other words, it tells how, given the initial state of affairs, the hero arrived at the final one.

In Schmidt's opinion, his narrative interrelation of events is also a structure of cause and effect, or ground and consequence, an important point to which I return at the end of this chapter. The story is told from a fiercely partisan attitude. Such partisanship is common in literary histories. I emphasize that literary history can use

---

[2] Julian Schmidt, *Geschichte der Deutschen Literatur seit Lessings Tod*, 5th ed. (Leipzig: Friedrich Grunow, 1866) 1:v–vi.

only traditional forms of narrative. For reasons to be
explored later, modernist forms of narration have not
been exploited in literary history and cannot be adapted
to its purposes.

The thread of events making up the narrative is selected from a much more capacious, amorphous past that
is known to the literary historian. We could argue that
the intention organizing a literary history justifies its
omissions and its emphases. But whatever the intention,
to a reader who knows the material as well as the literary
historian and, of course, to the literary historian himself,
any narrative will seem incomplete and somewhat arbitrary. For any event can be placed within many different
narrative sequences, long term and short. To represent
the past and to explain it as fully as our knowledge would
allow, we would have to make more sequences intersect
than is possible in traditional narrative form.

Desires, conscious and unconscious, play their role in
narrative literary history. That our emotions find satisfactions in writing (and reading) literary history is almost
too obvious to be mentioned. The question is, how much
do emotions shape the plot of its narratives? My point is
not that desire should not play a role — a neutral, blood-
less literary history, supposing this were possible, does
not represent my ideal. If I have anything to advocate on
the topic of desire, it is only common morality; that is, literary historians should be conscious of whatever desires
motivate them and should ask themselves whether or
not these desires are ones they wish to gratify.

Some of the issues can be posed by thinking, for example, of the many histories of modernist literature that tell
how the hero conquered the nineteenth century or of similar accounts of the revolt of romanticism against neoclas-
sic convention. David Daiches observes that the Georgian
poets of England in the 1910s lacked "vigor" and "had
nothing very new to say." T. S. Eliot "threw out the dregs
of the nineteenth century" ("worn-out conventions . . .
stock themes and attitudes, exhausted symbols"), gave

English poetry "a new vitality," and "reintroduced intelligence to the reading of poetry."[3] James E. B. Breslin
shapes the same story about poetry in the United States
in a subsequent period, the late 1950s and early 1960s:
"By mid-century American poetry had lost this destruc-
tive-creative energy" and had become timid and comfort-
able; but then, "many young poets . . . stretching poetic
language . . . made American poetry once again become
critical, passionate, innovative—alive."[4]

Such extreme partisanship seems to me uncritical. It
involves identification with one generation, aggression
against a former generation, and the narrator's vicarious
glory in the triumph of his chosen side. But to many readers it will seem appropriate for a literary historian to be
strongly partisan because he thus brings out the perspective of the writers who are his subject. Moreover, Fredric
Jameson is doubtless right that a degree of partisanship is
inevitable in narrative history: "Even in the study of the
past, *in so far as it is told as a story,* we are obliged by the
very form itself to take sides." The reader is compelled
into complicity "by the mechanism of point of view."[5] A
plot with clear heroes and villains, with the heroes mag-
nified by an admiring point of view, and with a victorious
combat in which the narrator participates emotionally is
a simple, well-known type, with many exemplars in western films and other romances. I would prefer more complicated plots for literary histories, but some plot there
certainly must be.

However, the issue I raise is different from the ones
just touched on, and it possibly goes deeper. The quota-
tions from David Daiches and James E. B. Breslin could

[3] David Daiches, *Poetry and the Modern World* (Chicago: U of Chicago P, 1940) 38, 109–11.

[4] James E. B. Breslin, "Poetry," in *Columbia Literary History of the
United States,* ed. Emory Elliott et al. (New York: Columbia UP, 1987)
1099.

[5] Fredric Jameson, *Marxism and Form: Twentieth-Century Dialectical Theories of Literature* (Princeton: Princeton UP, 1971) 262.

be multiplied as much as one liked, for such partisanship and simplification are very common in literary histories. They are striking and curious in persons whose training and metier as academic critics would lead one to expect a more complex view. It is also interesting that the attacks continue long after the battle is over. Though I just suggested some explanations, I would also ask whether literary histories are shaped by the pleasures of aggression and other emotional gratifications. Are literary historians eager to exorcise the hackneyed, genteel, and timid in themselves? Do they use as scapegoats the writers they condemn? On the other hand, the many literary historians who adopt an opposite role, championing styles that are currently neglected or unappreciated, may be motivated by a different, more chivalrous set of emotions. "Passions spin the plot," as George Meredith observes in his well-known sonnet. And what role does desire play in determining whether or not an interpretation of literary history will be accepted by readers?

Fantasies abound concerning the rise of the novel. George Saintsbury says that "from every point of view, high and low, serious and satiric, this Cinderella of literature has become the favourite princess";[6] and Joseph Boone, changing its gender, compares the novel to a beggar who becomes a king and has "the last laugh over its original detractors."[7] Literary history is and perhaps must be written in metaphors of origins, emergence from obscurity, neglect and recognition, conflict, hegemony, succession, displacement, decline, and so forth. Thus it activates archetypal emotions. Some literary history draws on psychic material in an unusually direct fashion. The theories of Harold Bloom that interpret literary history as oedipal struggle are themselves often interpreted as a

[6] George Saintsbury, *The Later Nineteenth Century* (London: William Blackwood, 1923) 65.

[7] Joseph Allen Boone, *Tradition Counter Tradition: Love and the Form of Fiction* (Chicago: U of Chicago P, 1987) 4.

projection of oedipal conflicts. The more we explore this topic, the more we would be speculating about the unconscious, with its drives and defenses. To the extent—this is my point—that narrative literary history is shaped by desires, we must suspect its plausibility as a description of the past.

Whatever the particular plot that is imposed on events, the mere fact that events are organized into narrative form may of itself fulfill desire. Hayden White points out that narrative form confers ideality and moral meaning on the events it interrelates and thus assures us that we do not live in a meaningless world.[8] Nietzsche says that we have art in order not to perish of the truth, and perhaps we have histories for the same reason. Donald Spence, reflecting on psychoanalysis, concludes that it is not possible to obtain historical truth, that is, to recover through analysis repressed traumatic events in the past, and that for therapeutic results, narrative truth—the continuity, closure, and plausibility of a good story—may be what matters. "Making contact with the actual past may be of far less significance [for therapy] than creating a coherent and consistent account of a particular set of events."[9] "The notion," says White, "that sequences of real events possess the formal attributes of the stories we tell about imaginary events could only have its origin in wishes, daydreams, reveries."[10]

But there is a counterargument. Narrative history differs fundamentally from fiction because, in constructing a novel, the "plot" takes precedence over the "story." The novelist will imagine events at the "story" level if they are required by the "plot." In writing narrative literary his-

[8] Hayden White, "The Value of Narrativity in the Representation of Reality," *Critical Inquiry* 7 (1980): 24. Reprinted in Hayden White, *The Content of the Form* (Baltimore: Johns Hopkins UP, 1987).

[9] Donald P. Spence, *Narrative Truth and Historical Truth* (New York: W. W. Norton, 1982) 27–28.

[10] White, "The Value of Narrativity" 27.

tory, one cannot do this. That we can make many different narratives out of the same events does not mean that the structure of events in our narrative is not true of the past. Any historical narrative will preserve the succession of events as they happened in the past; in other words, events will be said to have occurred in the chronological order that they actually did, so far as this can be determined, and a historical narrative may also preserve relations of cause and effect, antecedent and consequence, that pertained among events in the past, for our inferences about these relationships may be correct.

In this case, the narrative is not one we impose on the past but one that we draw from it, as an incomplete but not otherwise incorrect representation of the past. That a narrative of the past is selective and incomplete cannot mean that it is false, for if we granted this, the only faithful account of the past would be the past itself, and we would not regard this as a history. As Arthur Danto says, "Not being what it is a picture of is not a defect in pictures."[11] That our historical narratives gratify desires does not prove that they are misrepresentations, for the emotional satisfactions we get from a story have no relation to the criteria by which we estimate its truth.[12]

Traditional narratives have beginnings, endings, and plots that connect these points. They seem coherent. In fictional narratives, these features and their integration are appreciated as elements of a work of art. In history and literary history, they are equally artificial, but this is more difficult to admit, since it calls into question the credibility of the history as a representation of the past.

[11] Arthur C. Danto, *Narration and Knowledge* (New York: Columbia UP, 1985) 114.

[12] For suggestive discussion bearing on these points, see Christopher Prendergast, *The Order of Mimesis* (Cambridge: Cambridge UP, 1986) 41–42, 235; Paul Ricoeur, vol. 1, *Time and Narrative*, trans. Kathleen McLaughlin and David Pellauer (Chicago: U of Chicago P, 1984); for a discussion of Ricoeur, White, *The Content of the Form* 171–73.

Of beginnings, the artifice is obvious. Each "particular thought," as Wordsworth remarks, "hath no beginning,"[13] and the commencement of a literary history is a line drawn across the flow of a river. "The point of departure chosen by the historian," says Brandes, "must always be described as arbitrary and fortuitous; he must trust to his instinct and critical faculty, or he will never make a beginning at all" (198). No one thinks that English romanticism actually began with the publication of the *Lyrical Ballads* in 1798 or German literature with the *Hildebrandslied;* these inaugural moments are conventional, and histories of the same literature may choose different starting points. Moreover, unlike writers of fictional narratives, literary historians do not usually determine the beginnings of their histories in relation to the middles or ends.

Nevertheless, the chosen starting point has a remarkable impact on the way the literary past is represented. For example, it is conventional in literary histories to describe, in summary fashion, the state of affairs just prior to the beginning of the story that is to be told. Since this must be done in a brief space, a diversity of styles and tendencies cannot be surveyed. Events subsequent to the inaugural moment, however, are narrated at length, and hence, their diversity can be recorded. In fact, narrative necessities (there must be a change; there must be a conflict) require this. Thus it often happens that a phase of relative synthesis or homogeneity is said to have preceded the period that is the subject of the book.

In an article on nineteenth-century realism, Marshall Brown contrasts the conflicts within this period with the more unified eighteenth century.[14] Ian Watt believes that the divided tendencies of the eighteenth century were preceded by a relatively homogeneous age.[15] According to

[13] William Wordsworth, *The Prelude,* ed. Ernest de Selincourt and Helen Darbishire (Oxford: Clarendon, 1959), bk. 2, lines 229–32.
[14] Marshall Brown, "The Logic of Realism,"*PMLA* 96 (1981): 224–41.
[15] Ian Watt, *The Rise of the Novel* (Berkeley: U of California P, 1957).

Susan Wolfson, "some students of Victorian disintegrations are tempted to describe the Romantic era as a lost age of 'universals.'"[16] This gives the basic plot of unity exploding into heterogeneity. If the history is to be of romanticism, the literature or world view of the eighteenth century will be described as a synthesis from which romanticism breaks away in many different directions. If the history is to be of the Enlightenment, the preceding period, the later Renaissance, acquires the attribute of relative homogeneity. Thus, whether a given period is seen as unified or heterogeneous may reflect a formal consideration. If the period is to be described at length, it must be variegated or heterogeneous; if it is to be presented briefly, it must be more homogeneous.

Usually the ending of a literary history is artificial in the same sense as the beginning. Occasionally the material provides a clear and dramatic close; the history of Elizabethan and Jacobean drama stops with the eighteen-year closing of the theaters in 1642. But usually the literary historian sees his logical subject—the gothic novel, for example, or "natural supernaturalism"—undergoing a series of sudden or gradual transformations and revivals, and it is not clear exactly when or whether its history has ended.

Hence, most literary histories close where they do for formal, narrative reasons—usually for climax. Wilhelm Scherer, for example, published his *History of German Literature* in 1883, but he ended it with the death of Goethe. "Only thus did I obtain a worthy close, that I did not wish to spoil by a glance at the last fifty years of our literature, which would have seemed a scattered and distracting appendix."[17]

The traditional, fictional narratives of the nineteenth

[16] Susan J. Wolfson, *The Questioning Presence* (Ithaca: Cornell UP, 1986) 26. Wolfson refers to Carol Christ's Introduction to *The Finer Optic* (New Haven: Yale UP, 1975).

[17] Wilhelm Scherer, *Geschichte der Deutschen Literatur* (Berlin: Weidmann, 1883) 723.

century are organized teleologically. In other words, the ending determines the final meaning of what has gone before, and the episodes are created and (after the first reading) read with the ending in mind.[18] Histories may be written in the same way. Dilthey cites Eduard Meyer, "who sees in Thucydides his ideal, because from the point last reached Thucydides constructs a chain of causes that have determined this final state of affairs. In the end lies the principle that selects and forms" what enters the history.[19] The same thing could be said of many literary histories. Ronald Bush's *The Genesis of Ezra Pound's Cantos* (1976), for example, takes the achieved, somewhat bewildering style of the *Cantos* in 1925 as the terminal point of its narrative, as the state of affairs to be explained, and the story he tells is designed to set forth the experiences and reasons that by stages led Pound to write in this style. Edmund Gosse's *From Shakespeare to Pope* (1885) is similarly teleological as it accounts for the mode of Pope by a chain of antecedent events, and presumably any narrative literary history in which the closing state of affairs is regarded as the question to be answered will have a similar structure; that is, there will be a sequence of episodes that are coherent, meaningful, and explanatory in relation to the end.

In most literary histories, however, the narrative structure is less tight, for the historian does not fix his eye throughout on a final circumstance—the Jamesian novel, the style of the *Cantos*—that he wishes to account for. One reason he does not lies in the rule of sympathy that is imposed on him. Literary history assumes, as part of its own justification, that the knowledge it provides

[18] For discussion, see Peter Brooks, *Reading for the Plot* (New York: Random House, 1985) 22, 93.

[19] Wilhelm Dilthey, *Der Aufbau der geschichtlichen Welt in den Geisteswissenschaften, Gesammelte Schriften* (Leipzig: Teubner, 1936) 7:272. Hans-Georg Gadamer, *Truth and Method* (New York: Crossroad, 1989) 179, remarks: "The ontological structure of history itself . . . is teleological, although without a telos."

about texts conduces to better understanding and appreciation of them. It would be paradoxical and, for most literary historians, dismaying if, after they had related texts to their time and place, the texts left them cold. Moreover, since most of the texts noticed in a literary history are thought to have considerable merit as literature, a literary historian is under an obligation to feel and express this. He must appreciate each of the varied texts, one succeeding another, that are described. At least to some degree, each must be presented as an end in itself, rather than as a way station on the march of literary history toward some other text, and this means that the narrative structure must be somewhat episodic.

The possible plots of narrative literary history can be reduced to three: rise, decline, and rise and decline. The reason for this is that the hero of a narrative literary history is a logical subject—a genre, a style, the reputation of an author—and the plots are limited to what actions or transitions can be predicated of such heroes. They cannot, for example, go on a quest or be tormented in a love triangle. Of course, their rise or decline usually involves conflict with other logical subjects, thus enhancing the interest of the narrative. Many literary histories present the rise of one protagonist and the decline of another, as in W. J. Bate's *From Classic to Romantic* (1946), which traces the conflict of the declining classic and rising romantic premises in the aesthetics and criticism of England in the eighteenth century.

These plots can be treated in different modes. For example, the rise of the novel might be epic, romance, or comedy. And the metaphors in which rise or decline can be expressed are extremely various: coming of age, gathering of forces, spring and autumn—as in Van Wyck Brooks, *The Flowering of New England, 1815–1865* (1936), and *New England: Indian Summer, 1865–1915* (1940)—oedipal rebellion, erotic seduction and fall, and so forth. Needless to say, the same happening can be viewed as either rise or decline, depending on the perspective of the liter-

ary historian. In the early part of this century, for example, the novel was in decline for Lukács, Auerbach, and
anyone who highly valued realism, but it was advancing
for Virginia Woolf and other critics strongly oriented
toward sophisticated technique.[20]

I have chosen at random two passages as examples of
narrative literary history. Readers will probably find them
disappointing, for as narrative they are not very interesting. However, they illustrate my main point: that narrative literary history cannot be wholly adequate as history
because it is narrative. But they also show that it cannot
be very gripping as narrative because it is also criticism
and history.

The first passage comes from the 1917 *The Cam-
bridge History of American Literature.* Written by Carl
Van Doren, it describes the beginnings of the novel in the
United States.

> The clear victory which the first great British novelists won
> over popular taste did not, for some years, make them masters
> of the colonial public. *Pamela,* indeed, was printed as early as
> 1744 in Philadelphia, by Benjamin Franklin, and in the same
> year in New York and in Boston. But the only other novels
> printed in America before the Declaration of Independence
> seem to have been *Robinson Crusoe* (1768), *Rasselas* (1768),
> *The Vicar of Wakefield* (1772), *Juliet Grenville* (1774), and
> *The Works of Laurence Sterne M.A.* (1774). Publishers, how-
> ever, were less active than importers, for diaries and library
> catalogues show that British editions were on many shelves.
> The Southern and Middle colonies may have read more nov-
> els than did New England, yet Jonathan Edwards himself,
> whose savage quarrel over the "licentious books" [possibly
> *Pamela,* among others] which some of the younger members
> "employed to promote lascivious and obscene discourse," was
> later enchanted by *Sir Charles Grandison.*
>
> Edwards did not relent in advance of the general public.
> After the Revolution the novel-reading habit grew, fostered

[20] Wallace Martin, *Recent Theories of Narrative* (Ithaca: Cornell
UP, 1986) 19.

by American publishers and cried out against by many moralists whose cries appeared in magazines side by side with moral tales. Nearly every grade of sophistication applied itself to the problem. It was contested that novels were lies; that they served no virtuous purpose; that they melted rigorous minds; that they crowded out better books; that they painted adventure too romantic and love too vehement, and so unfitted readers for solid reality; that, dealing with European manners, they tended to confuse and dissatisfy republican youth. In the face of such censure, native novelists appeared late and apologetically, armed for the most part with the triple plea that the tale was true, the tendency heavenward, and the scene devoutly American. Before 1800 the sweeping philippic of the older school had been forced to share the field of criticism with occasional efforts to distinguish good novels from bad. No critical game was more frequently played than that which compared Fielding and Richardson. Fielding got some robust preference, Smollet had his imitators, and Sterne fathered much "sensibility," but until Scott had definitely set a new mode for the world, the potent influence in American fiction was Richardson. The amiable ladies who produced most of these early novels commonly held, like Mrs Rowson, that their knowledge of life had been "simply gleaned from pure nature," because they dealt with facts which had come under their own observation, but like other amateurs they saw in nature what art had assured them would be there. Nature and Richardson they found the same. Whatever bias they gave this Richardsonian universe was due to a pervading consciousness of the sex which read their novels. The result was a highly domestic world, limited in outlook, where the talk was of careless husbands, grief for dead children, the peril of many childbirths, the sentiment and the religion which enabled women to endure their sex's destiny. Over all hangs the furious menace of the seducer, who appears in such multitudes that one can defend the age only by blaming its brutality less than the pathetic example of Clarissa Harlowe.[21]

[21] *The Cambridge History of American Literature*, ed. William P. Trent et al. (New York: Macmillan, 1917–18) 1:284–85.

Hayden White argues that a narrative history is constructed in three phases. Though his model does not correspond to the way history is actually written, it is helpful in analyzing the texts produced. I also draw on ideas of Paul Ricoeur, who somewhat criticizes and modifies White.[22] According to this model, the first stage in creating a literary history is to make a chronicle, that is, to list in chronological order the works and other events that fall within the relevant time span. Thus in our example, the author knows which novels were printed or imported and when in colonial America and, from diaries, which novels were read when and by whom.

In the second phase, the literary historian must shape a story within the chronicle. This involves choosing a hero or logical subject, of which the changing fortunes will be followed—the novel in colonial America. Starting and terminal points must be picked out for the story that is to be told. In our example, the story begins with a time when novels were not written and were hardly read in the future United States and concludes with an opposite state of affairs.

In the third phase, the author must emplot his story; in other words, he must identify it with some archetype already familiar to the reader so that the reader will recognize it as a story of a particular kind. For unless the reader can perceive it as a story of victory, defeat, reconciliation, or whatever, he will not find it significant. This interpretive emplotment both determines and is shaped by the author's selection of incident, that is, by his decisions as to which events in the chronology he will emphasize, represent, faintly mention, or omit. But emplotment is mainly created by metaphors. In the present instance, the story is obviously emplotted as one of conflict and victory—the gradually successful struggle of the novel against the moralistic ethos. The emplotment goes

[22] Hayden White, *Tropics of Discourse* (Baltimore: Johns Hopkins UP, 1978) 58–63, 83–85, 109–10; Ricoeur 166–68.

further, however, for the novel is implicitly feminized, and it overcomes moral resistance as a seductive temptress or enchantress.

It is in the emplotment that the narrative must become historically impoverished, that is, it must become a thin, inevitably misleading representation of the past. We know, for example, that the reception of the novel in colonial America involved many other forces and circumstances that favored and hindered, besides its own inherent appeal and the resistance of Puritanism and other religious/moral codes. But the other factors are ignored—for if they were included, they would disrupt the unity of the narrative—and a simple struggle between two combatants, the novel and the moralistic ethos, is represented. Once this narrative archetype is imposed, the novel must overcome the opposition by itself.

This is a further drastic restriction of focus. The erosion of the religious/moral ethos permitted novels to be read and written, and the spread of novel reading was perhaps a contributing cause and certainly a symptom of the weakening moral rigidities, but we know that the relaxation of this ethos had other historical causes that completely transcend the influence of novels. Of these other, extraliterary factors, which supported the favorable reception of novels by undermining the older strictness, literary history says nothing. Narrative literary history must reduce the complexity of the past or it would cease to be narrative.

Incidentally, we may observe that the ironic attitude of the narrator in this extract is determined by his own historical circumstances. The arguments of moralists against novels could be represented as powerful. Instead, their objections are briefly catalogued in a way that dismisses them from serious consideration. The women who wrote novels, and presumably believed in what they were doing, are dismissed as amiable ladies with little experience of life. If we ask why the rule of sympathy is here abrogated, we may note that the date of this literary history was 1917. The author could hardly take the moralistic objections to novels seriously, since he was living in a historical context in which novels had long since been recognized as important literature and was himself, later in his book, to praise novels in the highest terms. If he were writing today, he could hardly look down on the women novelists of the period in the same way, since women are now strongly interested in literature written by women and are actively seeking it out.

The next example of narrative literary history is taken from Matthew Arnold's essay on Wordsworth. Here the hero is Wordsworth's fame—more precisely, it is the number of his readers—which rises and declines, this being the plot. In explaining this change, Arnold reduces the complexity of the past exactly as in our previous example, for he attributes the waxing and waning of Wordsworth's readership (which had innumerable causes, including extraliterary ones) to two factors only: the presence or absence of other popular poets (Byron, Scott, Tennyson) and the authority of critics (Scott, Coleridge). As usual in narrative literary history, the point of view is omniscient, so much so that the narrator can even go inside Scott's mind.

> The death of Byron seemed, however, to make an opening for Wordsworth. Scott, who had for some time ceased to produce poetry himself, and stood before the public as a great novelist; Scott, too genuine himself not to feel the profound genuineness of Wordsworth, and with an instinctive recognition of his firm hold on nature and of his local truth, always admired him sincerely, and praised him generously. The influence of Coleridge upon young men of ability was then powerful, and was still gathering strength; this influence told entirely in favour of Wordsworth's poetry. Cambridge was a place where Coleridge's influence had great action, and where Wordsworth's poetry, therefore, flourished especially. But even amongst the general public its sale grew large, the eminence of its author was widely recognised, and Rydal Mount became an object of pilgrimage. I remember

Wordsworth relating how one of the pilgrims, a clergyman, asked him if he had ever written anything besides the *Guide to the Lakes.* Yes, he answered modestly, he had written verses. Not every pilgrim was a reader, but the vogue was established, and the stream of pilgrims came.

Mr. Tennyson's decisive appearance dates from 1842. One cannot say that he effaced Wordsworth as Scott and Byron had effaced him. The poetry of Wordsworth had been so long before the public, the suffrage of good judges was so steady and so strong in its favour, that by 1842 the verdict of posterity, one may almost say, had been already pronounced, and Wordsworth's English fame was secure. But the vogue, the ear and applause of the great body of poetry-readers, never quite thoroughly perhaps his, he gradually lost more and more, and Mr. Tennyson gained them. Mr. Tennyson drew to himself, and away from Wordsworth, the poetry-reading public, and the new generations. Even in 1850, when Wordsworth died, this diminution of popularity was visible.[23]

Even more clearly than the previous example, this shows that the function of narrative in literary history is explanation. As a narrative presents a transition in the fortunes of the protagonist, it also accounts for it, conveying not only what happened but why. The explanatory power is in the causal relationship of antecedent to subsequent events, as the critical opinions of Scott and Coleridge were, according to Arnold, causes of the growing fame of Wordsworth in the 1830s. Moreover, a literary history must, as Ricoeur points out, defend itself against rival explanations that are also possible. These rivals inhabit the mind of the historian, who weighs alternative narrative explanations, and very often they also exist outwardly, in the writings of other historians of the same past. "In this respect," Ricoeur says, "historians are in the situation of a judge: placed in the real or potential situa-

---

[23] Matthew Arnold, "Wordsworth," in *Essays in Criticism, Second Series* (London: Macmillan, 1888) 123–25. Arnold's essay was originally published in 1879.

tion of a dispute, they attempt to prove that one given explanation is better than another" (175). Narrative explanation is also, implicitly, an argument. For this reason, the narrative must be closed. Everything that is included must hang together. Otherwise the explanation becomes less convincing.

Most narrative literary history is weighed down by commentary. The reason for this is partly that literary history includes literary criticism. Both of our examples abound in evaluative phrases, and in a great many literary histories the narrative is disrupted and slowed by interpolated passages of critical analysis. For literary works have, obviously, a value in themselves that far transcends their value as sources of literary history. To write a history of the romantic ode, one uses odes as sources, whatever else one also does. But one cannot treat these odes as one might printed or manuscript sources for a history of the French Revolution. They cannot simply be dissolved into the flow of narrative history. Because they are aesthetic objects, they must be described in and for themselves. As R. S. Crane puts it, "The historian of the literary arts must therefore find ways of dealing with the individual works . . . that will do justice at once to their multiple historical relations and to their qualities as unique artistic wholes."[24] In writing narrative literary history, this dilemma becomes a practical conflict between the opposed claims of two aesthetic forms, the literary work one is describing and the narrative one is constructing. The first requires pause for critical responsiveness; the second, coherence and momentum.

But the profusion of commentary in narrative literary history also has another cause. It is necessitated by the explanatory function of the narrative and by the wish of the literary historian to persuade us (and himself) that

---

[24] R. S. Crane, *Critical and Historical Principles of Literary History* (Chicago: U of Chicago P, 1971) 46.

the explanation offered is correct. These considerations lead him to bolster its credibility by arguments. Commentary may be inserted in order to show, for example, that an event did indeed happen as reported or that the significance assigned to it is correct. Though the narrator in our example knows that Scott praised Wordsworth, he nevertheless gives reasons for thinking that he would. And he similarly states arguments to support his judgment, which he gives as a narrative fact, that Tennyson did not efface Wordsworth.

Why, then, does narrative literary history not interest us strongly as narrative? Even the great literary histories of the nineteenth century, the readability of which I praised at the start of this chapter, are naturally much less pleasurable than nineteenth-century novels. If the reasons were only that literary histories cannot usually offer exciting incidents, intriguing characters, and suspenseful plots, the question would be trivial because its answer is obvious. The amount of commentary in literary histories is a second reason, and a third reason lies in the closure of narrative literary history. If we ask why narrative closure reduces interest, we find the best answer in considering the role of the reader, especially as this has been investigated by Wolfgang Iser.

A successful narrative, says Iser, activates attention and imagination by "gaps" or "unwritten portions," which the reader must fill in by conjecturing, by being himself creative. It includes events that are not definitively integrated with others by the narrator and that therefore summon the reader to complete this task. It contains details that cannot be fitted in at all and that continue to provoke the reader's powers by undoing whatever consistent construction he has briefly entertained—for as readers we always strive for consistency. As Iser puts it, "If the reader were given the whole story, and there were nothing left for him to do, then his imagination would never enter the field, the result would be the boredom which inevita-

bly arises when everything is laid out cut and dried before us."[25] But narrative literary history, intent on explaining the events it portrays, must leave the reader's imagination less scope. It does not and can not give the whole
story, as the examples we analyzed abundantly illustrate.
But all that it does give must hang together. Events that
do not cohere do not explain each other. Interpretations
that are potentially open must be closed by argument.

This is why narrative literary history cannot use the
techniques of modernist and postmodernist fiction. Generally speaking, these techniques have been developed in
opposition to traditional, linear narrative and closure.
They problematize such narratives, expose them as mere
artifice, deny their claim to be explanatory. And they do
this on the basis of an interpretation of life that emphasizes the truth of incoherence and inexplicability. From
this point of view, plot is the "alibi"—the words are Christopher Prendergast's—"which saves us from having to
live the contingency and randomness of the world" (231).

But though the world may indeed have this character,
narrative literary history has not reflected it up until
now. And it will not reflect it in the future, unless it surrenders its aspiration to explain. For from the point of
view of narrative as explanation, "if an earlier event is not
significant with regard to a later event in a story, it does
not belong in that story." I am quoting Arthur Danto, a
philosopher who emphatically believes that narrative history is possible. If, continues Danto, "every pair of events
mentioned in a story are so unrelated that the earlier one
is not significant with regard to the later one, the result
is in fact *not* a story" (134). That is, it is not history. Here
again we may note the conflict, in the writing of history
and literary history, between the need to describe the past
plausibly and the need to explain it. The first requires a

---

[25] Wolfgang Iser, *The Implied Reader: Patterns of Communication
in Prose Fiction from Bunyan to Beckett* (Baltimore: Johns Hopkins UP,
pbk., 1978) 275.

receptivity, at the very least, to multiplicity, heterogeneity, and randomness; the second requires that we resist these perceptions.[26]

As a final topic, we may notice what may be called conceptual literary history, since this mode of narrative organizes and interconnects events in an especially powerful way. For it exhibits the interrelation of events as the logical relations of ideas. Conceptual literary history is the mode that views the eighteenth century as the Age of Reason and displays eighteenth-century texts as particular moments of this idea. When literary histories cover more than one period, they may integrate each successive period under a different concept. These concepts might be quite unrelated to each other, as would be the case in literary histories that were strongly influenced by Foucault's theory that history jumps from one episteme to another. But usually the concepts organizing successive periods have a logical interconnection, as in the typical sequence, the Enlightenment (reason), romanticism (imagination and feeling), realism.[27] The logical structure of the organizing concepts presents the succession of periods as not only historical, but also intelligible — as something that can be understood and explained. In other words, on the basis of the conceptual relationships, the historian elaborates a scheme of historical change as simple reaction, dialectical process, cyclic, alternation between poles, or whatever.

Of course, change can also be represented as the dialectical development of a single idea, as in the Hegelian model. One of the splendid feats of Julian Schmidt's *History of German Literature since the Death of Lessing*

---

[26] Closure is necessary to explanation because, as Louis O. Mink puts it, "the force of explanation lies in the recognition of necessity" ("History and Fiction as Modes of Comprehension," *New Directions in Literary History*, ed. Ralph Cohen [Baltimore: Johns Hopkins UP, 1974] 109. The entire article is relevant to my argument).

[27] Crane (29–33) comments at some length on this type of literary history.

(1866) is to display the history of German literature as the unfolding of a political and ethical ideal. Thus he both unifies the texts under a concept and also integrates the long temporal span he surveys. Georg Lukács's *The Theory of the Novel* (1916) also conflates the dialectical development of an idea with the course of events in the past.

A similar dialectic may be perceived within periods. Rolf Grimminger exhibits the development of literature in the German Enlightenment as the dialectic of the idea of reason.[28] Michael McKeon's *The Origins of the English Novel, 1600–1740* is another example. McKeon views the method of Ian Watt on the same subject as organic; in other words, one concept, that of individualism, is said by Watt (in McKeon's account of Watt) to link developments in different lines of activity in England in the early eighteenth century—in philosophical discourse, in socioeconomic life, in the Protestant Reformation, and in narrative form, the latter being, of course, Watt's primary concern. In contrast, McKeon adopts a dialectical method.[29]

McKeon's model is complicated, and I shall set forth only a part of it, since my purpose is only to illustrate his procedure in literary historiography. He argues that in the latter part of the seventeenth century, narrative was involved in an epistemological crisis. The question was "how to tell the truth in narrative." From the discourse of the period, McKeon abstracts or categorizes three contending epistemologies: (1) "romance idealism," characterized by "a dependence on received authorities and a priori traditions"; (2) "naive empiricism"; and (3) "extreme skepticism," which is a skepticism about the claims to truth

[28] Rolf Grimminger, "Aufklärung, Absolutismus und bürgerliche Individuen: Über den notwendigen Zusammenhang von Literatur, Geselschaft und Staat in der Geschichte des 18. Jahrhunderts," *Hansers Sozialgeschichte der Deutschen Literatur vom 16. Jahrhundert bis zur Gegenwart*, vol. 3, *Deutsche Aufklärung bis zur Französischen Revolution 1680–1789*, ed. Rolf Grimminger (Munich: Carl Hanser, 1980).

[29] Michael McKeon, *The Origins of the English Novel, 1600–1740* (Baltimore: Johns Hopkins UP, 1987) 2, 20.

of the first two. These concepts have a dialectical relationship to each other, in that (2) is the negation of (1), and (3) the negation and synthesis of (1) and (2). For in negating (2), (3) adopts the same premises as (2) and carries them further, and it also "recapitulates some features of the romance idealism which it is equally committed to opposing." McKeon then conflates this dialectical interplay of concepts with the actual course of events in the past: (1) is chronologically the earlier epistemology, (3) the later one; the scheme represents phases by which the novel originated (20–21).

If we believe, as many say they do, that the satisfactions of literary history can only be aesthetic and intellectual, a conceptual history has obvious merits and no serious disadvantages. The tight coherence of such literary histories gives aesthetic pleasure, and the concepts themselves may be interesting. But if we hold that literary history should strive for a plausible representation of the past, we make a different evaluation. Any conceptual scheme highlights only those texts that fit its concepts, sees in texts only what its concepts reflect, and inevitably falls short of the multiplicity, diversity, and ambiguity of the past.

Though he greatly admires Hegel, Dilthey remarks that the "manifoldness of historical life is petrified in Hegel's dialectical method,"[30] and Lukács, looking back at his youthful work *The Theory of the Novel* in a 1962 introduction, admits that the book puts the novels it discusses into a "conceptual straightjacket."[31] To put it another way, any conceptual scheme can be undermined by positivistic citations of particular fact. And, of course, its concepts can always be criticized from the point of view of historical relativism. They have no validity transcending the time and place that produced them.

[30] Wilhelm Dilthey, *Der Aufbau der geschichtlichen Welt in den Geisteswissenschaften* (Frankfurt a. M.: Suhrkamp, 1970) 192.

[31] Georg Lukács, *The Theory of the Novel*, trans. Anna Bostock (Cambridge: MIT P) 13.

3

The Postmodern Encyclopedia

WE HAVE SOPHISTICATED CONCEPTIONS OF THE past, but no adequate form in which to convey them. The two major forms of literary history are the encyclopedic and narrative. They are not opposites, since narrative is a way of combining events, while encyclopedic form is a way of arranging essays to make a larger work. The essays may include narrative along with exposition and logical argument. Traditional narrative interrelates and unifies; the encyclopedia can be comprehensive precisely because it does not. Encyclopedic literary histories are sometimes called surveys, and might also be called compilations or aggregates. In histories of this type it is usually assumed that the authors and works discussed can be collected into period styles, and it is also assumed that they are part of a unified development, but neither the "family resemblances" between them nor the development are emphasized. Instead, the book is essentially a series of separate essays on separate authors or works, arranged in chronological order. Of the major forms, this can be either the most sophisticated or the least.

In the past, encyclopedic form has usually been adopted naively. The authors of these books have not reflected on the formal problems of literary history, do not understand the advantages of their form, and therefore, do not exploit them systematically. As a typical example, we can discuss Ifor Evans's *English Poetry in the*

Later Nineteenth Century (1933). In the preface, Evans says that he is offering a "continuous account of later nineteenth-century poetry,"[1] but except for his introduction, which takes an overview of the whole period, he does not do this at all. Continuity, or development, is represented almost solely in the fact that most of the chapters are printed in an order determined in part by chronology. Evans does not interrelate his poets but isolates each in a separate chapter, and when he combines very minor poets into one chapter (e.g., "Coventry Patmore and Allied Poets"), he still takes up each minor poet separately within the chapter. While discussing one poet, Evans almost never thinks of another poet; he places each singly under the bell jar of his examination. Thus, each of his discussions might as readily have been published as an encyclopedia article as in his book. Books of this kind are legion.

Encyclopedic form is free. The writer can put in whatever information or type of analysis that may help explain the problem he is addressing. Hence, works in encyclopedic form may mix biography, bibliography, intellectual history, social history, information about the reception of works, and criticism, moving from one to another with a flexibility that cannot easily be matched in narrative history. When a literary history has no plot, nothing appears as a digression.

But the great advantage of encyclopedic form is its conspicuous difference from our notions of reality. When we read narrative history, we may be tempted to suppose that the form of the discourse represents a — or even the — form in which events occurred in the past. But no one thinks the form of a past happening was encyclopedic, and the more encyclopedic the form — for example, the *Oxford Companion to English Literature*, with its entries arranged from *A* to *Z* — the less can we mistake it for the

---

[1] B. Ifor Evans, *English Poetry in the Later Nineteenth Century* (London: Methuen, 1933) ix.

form of the past. To put the point another way, what all discursive form actually is, encyclopedic form obviously is, a form erected alongside the unknowable form of reality. Like any form, it distorts the past as it presents it, but that the past is distorted is, in encyclopedic form, blatant, even if we do not have in mind an alternative form that the past might be given.

Or we might even say, encyclopedic form does not distort the past at all, for in it the events that make up the past are not interrelated in a determined way. If we are presented with separate essays, we must connect them for ourselves in our own minds and can explore different possibilities of doing so. Thus the encyclopedic can be a relatively open form of literary history. It is especially appropriate, not only practically but intellectually, that literary histories in encyclopedic form are often written by a committee, as in the *Cambridge History of English Literature.* In such works, each author contributes a chapter on his specialty, and the inconsistencies between one essay and another that may thus arise are possibly not to be regretted.

Encyclopedic form can be an attempt to embody our sense of the overwhelming multiplicity and heterogeneity of the past (any tract of the past), of the points of view that can be brought to bear, of the hypotheses that can structure the same events, and of the morals that can be drawn from them. This sense of history characterizes postmodern theory but is not necessarily new. It was already present in Germany during the romantic period and was expressed in England by Carlyle, who had a quasi-mystical perception of the infinite interrelations, transcending all possibility of knowledge, of one event with all: "It is not in acted, as it is in written History: actual events are nowise so simply related to each other as parent and offspring are; every single event is the offspring not of one, but of all other events, prior or contemporaneous . . . it is an ever-living, ever-working Chaos of Being, wherein shape after shape bodies itself forth from innumerable elements."[2] Of course, Carlyle still assumes that actual history is continuous. If, instead, we make the post-modern supposition that actual history is not only an "ever-working Chaos" but also discontinuous, we have the sense of the past that can make the encyclopedic seem not the most naive form of literary history, but the most sophisticated.

As an example of an attempt to use encyclopedic form in a sophisticated way, we may consider the 1987 *Columbia Literary History of the United States*. This volume has sixty-six essays, each by a different contributor. In the general introduction, the editor explains that the book is not committed to anything it says, since a statement in one essay may be contradicted in another. This fact is interpreted as "postmodern: it acknowledges diversity, complexity, and contradiction by making them structural principles, and it forgoes closure as well as consensus."[3] Taking Eliot and Pound for examples, we find, by using the index, that for several contributors they were "avant-garde" and "experimental" poets, but for James M. Cox they were "regionalists," whose "form, its attendant emotion, and . . . enterprise" were "the essence of the middle-class American artist" (776).

For Cary Nelson, in an article on "The Diversity of American Poetry," Eliot and Pound were racists and anti-Semites (930), and the relations between Pound's "despicable" broadcasts from Rome and his *Cantos* have been "long suppressed by academic critics" (935). The essay in this volume by Walton Litz on "Ezra Pound and T. S. Eliot" must, for Nelson, illustrate this suppression, since it mentions racism and anti-Semitism very briefly and gently.

Neither is the *Columbia Literary History* committed

---

[2] Thomas Carlyle, "On History," in *Critical and Miscellaneous Essays* (New York: AMS, 1969) 2:88.

[3] *Columbia Literary History of the United States*, ed. Emory Elliott et al. (New York: Columbia UP, 1987) xiii.

to its own form. The volume organizes its material into five chronological periods, but these demarcations are only for "convenience." Although the table of contents suggests a traditional survey narrative, this impression is misleading, and the active formal principle is discontinuity: "In contrast to the 1948 volume, we [the editors] have made no attempt to tell a 'single, unified story' with a 'coherent narrative.' . . . No longer is it possible, or desirable, to formulate an image of continuity" (xxi). But the editors do not really mean this, perhaps because they do not want to close the possibility that literature develops continuously, and so they recommend that readers find continuities by using the index selectively: "Reading selectively, a person may also trace the development of religious and philosophical thought. . . . Similarly, selective study of the essays devoted to particular genres will provide a survey of the developments of poetry, drama, criticism, and the novel over time. The index is a guide to such continuous as well as multiple treatments" (xxi). And although the editors concede that the "distinction of its publisher and its imposing title may suggest authority," the *Columbia Literary History of the United States* is "not an authoritative proclamation" (xxiii). In fact, "in important ways . . . the reader of the work will always be involved in an act of creating his or her own interpretations of the literary history of the United States by combining related essays" (xxi).

In *A New History of French Literature* (1989), the deconstruction of traditional literary history goes even further. This book is also made up of articles by writers with varying interests and points of view. The articles are arranged in chronological order, according to their subject matter, but in contrast with the *Columbia Literary History of the United States*, the topics of the articles are in many cases not the informative surveys one expects to find in literary histories. Instead, the editor, Denis Hollier, and his contributors have devised highly focused topics that illuminate specialized questions while leaving a great deal in the dark. Thus there is no essay on the works, achievement, and place in history of Proust, but there is an essay on his theory of art in relation to his consciousness of death, and in other essays, there are occasional, passing mentions of Proust in connection with the Dreyfus affair, with Gide on homosexuality, and so on. A reader who acquired his information only from *A New History of French Literature* would not know why Proust is a topic at all.

Since this work presupposes that the reader has much information already, the audience it tacitly has in mind is a limited one, composed mainly of specialists in French literature and theorists of literary history. A literary history of this type is logically ancillary or supplemental to Gustave Lanson's *Histoire de la littérature française* (1895) or to similar sources of information. There must be a positive construction of literary history before there can be the deconstruction that characterizes the next stage in historical sophistication.

The choice and arrangement of topics in *A New History of French Literature* deliberately dismantles the "concept of *period*."[4] This is done by the particularity of the topics and the different perspectives of the essays, which are such that if there were periods, they would subsume multiple, radically heterogeneous, discontinuous happenings. It is also done by juxtaposing topics that refer to different durations; we jump from the long to the short term and back. The editor explains that "rather than following the usual periodization schemes by centuries, as often as possible we have favored much briefer time spans and focused on nodal points, coincidences, returns, resurgences" (xx). Even more deconstructive is the "fragmentation" (xx) of the concept of author: "No article is conceived as a comprehensive presentation of a single author" (xix). Instead, there are brief discussions or men-

---

[4] *A New History of French Literature*, ed. Denis Hollier (Cambridge: Harvard UP, 1989) xx.

tions in different contexts of particular activities of an author or aspects of his or her work.

To emphasize that historical reality is an array of particulars, heterogeneous and unstructurable, is typical of postmodernist cultural criticism. It is also an extreme version of a mode of historical perception that, according to Karl Mannheim, characterizes a politically dominant class.

> A class which has already risen in the social scale tends to conceive of history in terms of unrelated, isolated events. Historical events appear as a process only as long as the class which views these events still expects something from it. . . . [With] success in the class struggle . . . there appears a picture of the world composed of mere immediate events and discrete facts. The idea of a "process" and of the structural intelligibility of history becomes a mere myth.[5]

In *A New History of French Literature,* individual essays use historical context in different ways and degrees and in this, as in other respects, they are often extremely sophisticated. The contextualizing involved in the formal arrangement of the whole is deeply ironical and almost whimsical. The essays are arranged by date, and "each date is followed by a 'headline,' evoking an event" (xix). In other words, each essay is juxtaposed to a bit of historical context, an occurrence in literary life, political reality, and so on. Thus allusively invoked, the piece of context is only a fragment of the total context (which can never be described anyway) and has, moreover, no intrinsic or important connection with the topic it contextualizes. It "specifies not so much the essay's content as its chronological point of departure. . . . The juxtaposition of these events is designed to produce an effect of heterogeneity and to disrupt the traditional orderliness of most histories of literature" (xix).

In their size, the prestige of their publishers, the scope

[5] Karl Mannheim, *Ideology and Utopia: An Introduction to the Sociology of Knowledge* (New York: Harcourt, Brace, 1936) 129–30.

of their subjects, and the reputation of their contributors, the *Columbia Literary History of the United States* and the *New History of French Literature* are the two most important literary histories that have appeared recently in the United States. Both are intended to respond to a genuine crisis in literary historiography. Their forms of presentation are evidence of the crisis and also show why this formal model cannot overcome it. Encyclopedic form is intellectually deficient. Its explanations of past happenings are piecemeal, may be inconsistent with each other, and are admitted to be inadequate. It precludes a vision of its subject. Because it aspires to reflect the past in its multiplicity and heterogeneity, it does not organize the past, and in this sense, it is not history. There is little excitement in reading it.

4

Literary Classifications:
How Have They Been Made?

CLASSIFICATION IS FUNDAMENTAL TO THE DISCI-
pline of literary history. A literary history cannot have
only one text for its subject, and it cannot describe a great
many texts individually. The multiplicity of objects must
be converted into fewer, more manageable units, which
can then be characterized, compared, interrelated, and
ordered.

Classifications map the cultural world. Literature by
blacks in the United States can be a separate taxonomic
unit, or it can be integrated with literature by whites.
Langston Hughes can be placed in the same group with
Amiri Baraka or with Carl Sandburg. The tendency in
German literary histories to demarcate a literary period
by the Third Reich has, Alexander von Bormann says, a
"perceptibly disburdening function." The period falls "out
of our cultural tradition as an exotic," ceases to be
"'present past.' This changes at once if one proceeds from
the thesis of continuity, and pays attention to the many
lines of connection."[1] Thus, classifications shape our
sense of national and personal identity.

The importance of literary taxonomy to the profes-

---

[1] Alexander von Bormann, "Zum Umgang mit dem Epochenbe-
griff," in *Literatur und Sprache im historischen Prozeß. Vorträge des
Deutschen Germanistentages Aachen 1982*, ed. Thomas Cramer, vol. 1,
Literatur (Tübingen: Max Niemeyer, 1983) 191.

sion cannot be overstated. Classifications are organizing principles of courses (The Lyric), library shelves (Fiction: American — Nineteenth Century), societies (the divisions of the Modern Language Association), journals (*Studies in Romanticism*), anthologies, collections of essays, conferences, and tenure searches. They are used and contested in struggles for institutional power.

We might argue, with Croce, that we can classify texts any way we like, since the label will not change our actual experience in reading. In this last point I am sure that he is wrong, for a classification brings with it a context of other works. If we change the context, we activate a different system of expectations, of hermeneutic fore meanings. When we group texts together, we emphasize the qualities they have in common and ignore, to some degree, those that differentiate them. If "Lycidas" and "Adonais" are interconnected as pastoral elegies, this genre classification calls attention to certain formal features of the poems and not to their very unlike *Weltanschauungen*. Thus a classification is also an orientation, an act of criticism.

We may digress here to notice terminological difficulties. I have been using *classify* in a loose sense to refer to the process of distributing authors or works in the literary field into larger units — periods, genres, traditions, schools, movements, communicative systems — each containing many individuals. A classification is either one such unit or the ensemble of them. But if a literary critic wished to speak of English romantic poetry as a variety of poetry distinguished from other varieties, he would not call it a class of poetry, but a type. So also with many other categories into which we sort works. In the minds of writers and readers, they are entertained more as prototypes or sets of expectations than as classes.

The differences between groups, classes, and types is a topic of inveterate, continuing discussion in philosophy, sociology, and other fields; definitions are variable, and the problems, complicated and disputed. As literary theorists generally understand the term at present, a *class* is formed on the basis of features or sets of features that works have in common. In classifying, we direct a question or number of questions to works—do they have a narrator? are they in verse?—and sort them on the basis of the answers.

Literary works of the same *type* also have shared features, but the reason for collecting them together is that each individual work approximates a conceptual model of the type. The model may be vague, and the approximation may be more or less, and thus the works included in the type may vary from each other a good deal. A *group* is the vaguest and most general of the three terms, and in literary histories it usually refers to a number of persons who were personally connected with each other. Thus we speak of the Imagist group of poets. Of course, when we use *group* as a taxonomic term, we always assume that the personal interconnections of the writers led to similarities in their writings.

In analyzing the activities of literary historians, I shall speak of them as grouping, classifying, or assigning to types, using whichever term seems most appropriate to the particular act of sorting that is being inspected. But very often literary historians are engaged in grouping, classifying, and assigning to types simultaneously, so that no single term is adequate. As the preferred verb when no verb does better than another, I shall use *classify*, and this will also cover the whole, general process of assorting literary works.

Despite the importance of the topic, not much critical reflection has been focused recently in the United States on literary classification and its problems.[2] Furthermore,

---

[2] For genres, see Paul Hernadi, *Beyond Genre: New Directions in Literary Classification* (Ithaca: Cornell UP, 1972); Rosalie L. Colie, *The Resources of Kind: Genre-Theory in the Renaissance,* ed. Barbara K. Lewalski (Berkeley: U of California P, 1973); J. P. Strelka, ed., *Theories of Literary Genre* (University Park: Pennsylvania State UP, 1978); Alastair Fowler, *Kinds of Literature: An Introduction to the Theory of Genres and*

except in considerations of genre, discussion has been limited to only one question, namely, whether literary taxonomies can correspond to historical realities. The terms of this argument are not exactly the same with respect to periods, genres, traditions, movements, and other categories, but they are similar, and our thinking about periodization illustrates the state of the question with respect to literary classifications in general.

In *Theory of Literature* (1949), Wellek rejected both the notion that periods are metaphysical entities and the opposite opinion of Croce that periods are merely conventional. Adapting ideas of the Russian Formalists and Czech Structuralists, Wellek argued that a period is created by a dominant "system of literary norms, standards, and conventions." Thus Wellek secured the objectivity and relative unity of periods, while also allowing for a degree of heterogeneity and struggle within them.[3]

Modes (Cambridge: Harvard UP, 1982); Barbara K. Lewalski, ed., *Renaissance Genres: Essays on Theory, History, and Interpretation* (Cambridge: Harvard UP, 1986); Ralph Cohen, "History and Genre," *New Literary History* 17 (Winter 1986); Clifford Siskin, *The Historicity of Romantic Discourse* (New York: Oxford UP, 1988); and works on particular genres. For problems of taxonomy in general, see the very elegant discussion of eighteenth-century taxonomy in the natural sciences in Michel Foucault, *The Order of Things* (New York: Pantheon, 1970). For taxonomy and especially periodization in literary history, see R. S. Crane, *Critical and Historical Principles of Literary History* (Chicago: U of Chicago P, 1971); Claudio Guillen, *Literature as System* (Princeton: Princeton UP, 1971); Ulrich Weisstein, *Comparative Literature and Literary Theory: Survey and Introduction*, trans. William Riggan in collaboration with the author (Bloomington: Indiana UP, 1973); John Frow, *Marxism and Literary History* (Cambridge: Harvard UP, 1986). Among recent discussions in Germany of periodization, mention may be made of Uwe Japp, *Beziehungssinn: Ein Konzept der Literaturgeschichte* (Frankfurt a. M.: Europäische Verlagsanstalt, 1980); the essays by various writers in *Epochenschwellen und Epochenstrukturen im Diskurs der Literatur — und Sprachhistorie*, ed. H. U. Gumbrecht and Ursula Link-Heer (Frankfurt a. M.: Suhrkamp, 1985); Siegfried J. Schmidt, "On Writing Histories of Literature: Some Remarks from a Constructivist Point of View," *Poetics* 14 (Aug. 1985): 279–301.

   [3] René Wellek and Austin Warren, *Theory of Literature* (New York: Harcourt, Brace, 1949) 277–78.

Wellek's views were accepted, though not without criticism, by Guillen, Weisstein, Japp, and most others who wrote about the theory of literary history. This consensus lasted, though gradually weakening, until the beginning of the 1970s.

At present, we tend to regard periods as necessary fictions. They are necessary because, as the preceding paragraph illustrates, one cannot write history or literary history without periodizing. Moreover, we require the concept of a unified period in order to deny it, and thus make apparent the particularity, local difference, heterogeneity, fluctuation, discontinuity, and strife that are now our preferred categories for understanding any moment of the past.[4]

Our postmodernist questioning of the unity and objectivity of periods bases itself on the historiography of the *Annales* school and Lévi-Strauss's appendix to *The Savage Mind*, both stressing the overlap of long- and short-term events (these ideas already modified Guillen's view of literary periodization); the structuralist sense of systematic oppositions or differences within any field we discriminate; the genealogy of Foucault and its polemic against totalizations; the orientation to the history of reception, which yields periods quite different from those in the traditional literary history of the genesis of works;[5] the argument of hermeneutics that periods of the past are constructed from a present perspective and

[4] Harro Müller, "Einige Argumente für eine subjektdezentrierte Literaturgeschichtsschreibung," *Kontroversen, alte und neue. Akten des VII. Internationalen Germanisten-Kongresses Göttingen 1985*, vol. 11, *Historische und aktuelle Konzepte der Literaturgeschichtsschreibung. Zwei Königskinder? Zum Verhältnis von Literatur und Literaturwissenschaft*, ed. Albrecht Schöne (Tübingen: Max Niemeyer, 1986) 27, cites Françoise Gaillard's opinion that "exactly the admittedly impure movements of totalization are indispensable as constructive procedures, in order to be at all able to affirm breaks, leaps, diversities, and dispersions."

[5] Janusz Slawinski, "Reading and Reader in the Literary Historical Process," *New Literary History* 19 (Spring 1988): 526.

change as the present moves on; *Ideologiekritik,* emphasizing that classifications serve ideological interests; and the deconstructive and postmodern sense of local difference and interpretive undecidability.

Also, more traditional objections still have force. According to Croce, a work of art embodies an individual intuition and, hence, every work of art differs from all others. The literary field—any assemblage of texts that we wish to divide into groups—is always perfectly heterogeneous. When we classify texts, we put the continuously differing objects into a few pigeonholes.

We owe especially to Dilthey the concept that periods are spiritually or ideologically unified tracts of time, but even Dilthey worried that such representations are integral and stable, while life is endlessly diverse and changing. Periods are "fixed representations of something in progress, giving fixity in thought to that which in itself is process or movement in a direction."[6] When we speak of the romantic period, we isolate a duration within a longer duration and suggest, without wishing to do so, that the process of change ceases within the period. This point has frequently been noted by theorists of literary history,[7] and the same objection applies to concepts of schools and movements. The phrase "Imagist movement" suppresses not only the differences among the texts it synthesizes but also the development of this style over time, for a typical "Imagist" poem in the 1930s was unlike one in the 1910s. The previous sentence commits the errors it criticizes and thus illustrates the problem, which is rooted in the nature of conceptual thinking and language.

Theorists have proposed new taxonomic categories— horizon of expectations, discourse, communicative sys-

---

[6] Wilhelm Dilthey, *Der Aufbau der geschichtlichen Welt in den Geisteswissenschaften, Gesammelte Schriften,* 2d ed. (Stuttgart: Teubner, 1958) 7:157.

[7] Wellek and Warren 278; Guillen 445; Crane 28.

tem, episteme—that will, it is hoped, escape the objections to the traditional ones. But emphasis on particularity, difference, and discontinuity undermines confidence in all classifications. At the same time, of course, we must classify, since otherwise we sink into a mass of unrelated details and lose all possibility of understanding them. A typical idea at present is, then, that we must impose taxonomies but must not believe that they correspond to historical realities. Philippe Forget says that in writing a literary history one must "accept a definite division" of the material but, "in the course or at the end of the investigation," must also make the division appear "unsuitable" and give it up or restructure it.[8]

The interrelations of texts and authors in a literary history are not "embedded in the historical process" for the historian to discover, as Wellek maintained (278), but are constructed by the literary historian. "We must admit," says Siegfried Schmidt, "that we have to apply criteria other than truth, objectivity, or reliability to literary histories, and that we have to formulate social functions for literary histories other than that of providing a true report on 'what has been the case'" (285).

But this argument, replacing the consensus created by Wellek, still refers to the same question: can literary taxonomy represent the past? On this occasion I temporarily bracket this question in order to raise others we have not asked, or are only now beginning to ask, about literary classifications. These questions pertain to their provenance (who made them? how? with what interests or motives?), to their reception (who or what determines their acceptance? why and how do they change?), and to their functions in determining what we read, in modifying our responses to texts and our interpretations of

---

[8] Philippe Forget,"Literatur—Literaturgeschichte—Literaturgeschichtsschreibung: Ein rückblickender Thesenentwurf," in *Kontroversen, alte und neue. Akten des VII. Internationalen Germanisten-Kongresses Göttingen 1985*, vol. 11, ed. Schöne, 44.

them, in organizing the past, in careers and institutional life, and in society at large. These questions may be asked both about particular classifications and about the process of literary classification in general.

First I attempt to analyze how, by what processes, literary historians have classified, grouped, or assigned works to types. I try only to describe what have been and still are the usual methods and do not suggest what ought to be done instead. The investigation is empirical, in the sense that it concentrates on particular instances of literary historians at work. The difficulties of classification are, for literary historians, a relatively unexplored subject. Consciousness has not been raised about it. Naturally, therefore, in most literary histories the problem is handled naively, and the results seem more arbitrary and less convincing than is necessary. But whether naive or sophisticated, literary histories follow essentially the same procedures in classification, and the procedures are my topic, not their crude or elegant application. The examples are chosen almost at random, and my generalizations are based on studying many more instances than space allows to be analyzed. Another set of examples would not lead to different conclusions.

Obviously, the processes of literary taxonomizing have been contingent and the results irrational. They are not at all like the efforts of Linnaeus and other eighteenth-century naturalists described by Foucault in *The Order of Things*, for the naturalists, though often myopic in the criteria on which they based their classifications, were otherwise logical and systematic. Ideally speaking, a taxonomic system would observe the rules of logical division: the system of classification would be based on variations of the same features in each work; it would make it impossible to classify a text or author into more than one category; and every text or author would fit into one or another category—in other words, nothing we wish to classify would lack a place in the system. Literature has no taxonomic system, but only a confused aggregate of overlapping classifications from different points of view. To see how literary classifications have actually been made tells us why.

Literary classifications have been determined mainly by six factors: tradition, ideological interests, the aesthetic requirements of writing a literary history, the assertions of authors and their contemporaries about their affinities and antipathies, the similarities that the literary historian observes between authors and/or texts, and the needs of professional careers and the politics of power in institutions. This chapter does not analyze examples of the latter, for either the political and careeristic motives are glaringly obvious, or they are combined with more "acceptable," apparently "objective" ones.

In *American Renaissance*, for example, F. O. Matthiessen unified a number of writers who previously had seemed rather heterogeneous, and he evaluated them in a new, very positive way. This construction was not made for careerist reasons, and its favorable reception is not to be explained mainly on materialist grounds. But Matthiessen's construction promoted the interests of American studies as a discipline, and this is one reason why it was widely accepted. Contrary to what might naively be supposed, direct observation of texts is the most unusual method of classification, and it is also the least effective if effectiveness is measured by acceptance. Henceforth in this chapter, I attempt to give these generalizations concreteness and detail by studying particular cases. The most surprising thing such cases reveal to me is the overwhelming role of tradition in the process of taxonomizing.

We may begin by asking why the 1985 *Cambridge History of Classical Literature* divides Greek lyric poetry from the seventh to fifth centuries B.C. into the following categories: elegy and iambus, archaic choral lyric, monody (lyric for solo voice), and choral lyric in the fifth century. Whoever has to classify this poetry is not to be envied, since all that has survived are texts or significant fragments of approximately eighteen poets, widely scattered in time and place, about whom we have little and mostly unreliable information. But no one starting now from scratch to classify this verse would decide that the historical and other interrelations between these poets are best disclosed by a system based mainly on versification and on choral or solo mode of performance. Yet this is the organizing principle adopted in the *Cambridge History*, though the system also takes account of chronology. It does not reflect the different dialects in which the poems were written, their social uses, their provenance, or their subject matters, though we must admit that if we used these criteria, we would find it no less difficult to group the poems in historically meaningful ways.

The system in the *Cambridge History* is essentially the same as the first classification of these poets, which was made by Alexandrian grammarians in the third century B.C. They divided the poets of two to four centuries earlier into those who wrote in elegiac meter, those in iambic meter, and lyric poets (a term they invented), who wrote in stanzas. The Alexandrian canon was widely known in the ancient world, and descended through the Middle Ages and the Renaissance.[9] When the first works that we would recognize as literary histories were composed in the eighteenth century, they naturally adopted the Alexandrian scheme of classification. An example is the course of lectures given at Halle in the 1780s by F. A. Wolf, the famous scholar and teacher whose *Prolegomena ad Homerum* (1795) first raised the Homer question. In his lectures, Wolf discussed the melic (lyric), iambic, and elegiac poets separately, and within each classification, he followed chronological order. He frankly admitted that "it cannot and should not be avoided that a later author is mentioned before an earlier one in a different genre."[10]

---

[9] Weisstein (111, 120) summarizes the history of this taxonomy in the ancient world, though his information differs slightly from mine.

[10] Friedrich August Wolf, *Vorlesungen über die Altertumswissenschaft*, ed. J. D. Gurtler and S. F. W. Hoffmann, vol. 2, *Vorlesungen über*

Interesting early attempts to break away from the Alexandrian scheme of classification were made by Herder in his essay on "Alcaeus und Sappho" (1795) and by Friedrich Schlegel in "Von den Schulen der Griechen und Römer" (1798). They strove to create a taxonomy based on periods and schools. Herder distinguished a first period of Greek poetry characterized by epic and elegy and a second period of poetry of the type associated with Lesbos, the poetry of Alcaeus and Sappho. Schlegel attempted to make the different Greek tribes the basis of a taxonomy. He described an Ionian school, a Dorian school, and so forth, and in his *Geschichte der hellenischen Dichtkunst* (1838–39), G. H. Bode attempted to carry out Schlegel's idea in detail, making racial stock (*Volk*) the leading theme of his taxonomy. But this and similar attempts shattered on their own historical inaccuracy and internal inconsistency, and the hundreds of literary histories of Greece in the nineteenth century generally reverted to the Alexandrian classification, deploying four categories in two pairs: elegiac and iambic verse, choral and solo lyric.

Of course, classical literary historians argued that versification was regularly associated with other significant features, thus making their taxonomies seem less arbitrary. K. O. Müller, for example, maintained that "the Greek poets always chose their verse with the nicest attention to the feelings to be conveyed by the poem."[11] But his further exposition showed that Greek elegiac verses, for example, might express a great range of feelings—warlike, erotic, political, convivial, or lamenting. Müller was thus compelled to seek other essential features shared by poems in elegiac meter. These were, he said, strong emotion, "honest and straightforward expres-

die Geschichte der griechischen Literatur, ed. J. D. Gurtler (Leipzig: Lehnhold, 1839) 111.

[11] K. O. Müller and John William Donaldson, *A History of the Literature of Ancient Greece* (London: John W. Parker, 1858) 1:142.

sion," and a social use: elegies were sung at banquets (147).

In his *Grundriß der griechischen Literatur* (1836–45), Gottfried Bernhardy, who regarded Müller as superficial, sought to correlate verses in elegiac meter with the racial characteristics of the Ionian *Volk* that created the meter and with the historical emergence of individual self-consciousness. We need not follow these arguments in detail in order to see that the ancient classification by meter was causing embarrassment. Yet, as late as 1929, the authoritative Schmid-Stählin asserted that "the division according to *literary genres* . . . corresponds for the most part with the division according to racial stocks and dialects,"[12] a point that is denied by the 1985 *Cambridge History*.[13]

Thus, a dubious scheme of classification has lasted for more than two thousand years. We might argue that classical scholarship is a special case. It requires a long apprenticeship, and not many people can be involved. The issues are remote from the interests of the present. My point, however, is that classical scholarship is typical: the grip of tradition is powerful in all cases.

As we write literary histories, a scheme of classification is usually already in existence, as was true for F. A. Wolf and all of his successors. If literary historians think about these classifications, their thoughts have already been shaped by them. The classification is prior, in a sense, to the literature it classifies, for it organizes perceptions of the literature. The validity of the classification confirms itself every time the texts are read, for the clas-

---

[12] Wilhelm Schmid and Otto Stählin, *Geschichte der Griechischen Literatur, Erster Teil: Die klassische Periode der griechischen Literatur,* von Wilhelm Schmid. *Erster Band: Die griechische Literatur vor der attischen Hegemonie* (Munich: C. H. Beck'sche Verlagsbuchhandlung, 1929) 7: i, 9.

[13] *The Cambridge History of Classical Literature, I: Greek Literature,* ed. P. E. Easterling and B. M. W. Knox (Cambridge: Cambridge UP, 1985) 158.

sification signals what to look for and therefore predetermines, to some degree, what will be observed.

Imprinted taxonomies are also resistant to change for the simple reason that the number of ideas one has time and occasion to consider and correct is small in comparison to the total number of ideas one harbors. The content of anyone's mind consists mostly of received ideas, including the traditional taxonomies. It takes so much more energy, so much more knowledge and reflection, to disturb the received system than to accept and apply it, that anyone can revise it at only a few points. Hence, in any comprehensive literary history, the main source of taxonomies will be cultural transmission. To these considerations we may add the conservative influence of the audience. To the extent that readers already know the traditional taxonomies, they expect them in literary histories. A literary historian who proposes different taxonomies must make an argument.

Finally, so far as it is a logical process, taxonomizing involves reasoning in a hermeneutic circle. A literary taxonomy includes a name (e.g., modernism), a concept, and a canon of works subsumed under the concept. Reasoning goes from the concept to the canon, from the canon to the concept. Both may be modified, but before the process can start, they must be given. In most cases they are given by tradition, that is, by previously existing classifications of these texts. Very large modifications may take place over time, but the process can never completely transcend its beginnings.

Thus literary histories are made out of literary histories. Not only their classifications but also their plots are derived from previous histories of the same field. A literary history can be an accurate mimesis of the past only if all of the literary histories it echoes also are. The authority of a literary historian rests on other authorities, which are, in fact, no more authoritative than the present one. This realization is not new. In his *Defence of Poetry*, Sir Philip Sidney complained of the historian "laden with old mouse-eaten records, authorizing himself (for the most part) upon other histories, whose greatest authorities are built upon the notable foundation of hearsay."[14]

In one respect, however, the *Cambridge History of Classical Literature* differs from all previous classifications of ancient Greek lyric. It includes a category of "Women Poets." That the reasons for its inclusion are political and ideological is the more obvious because the category has little ground otherwise, few verses by women poets having survived. (The category does not include Sappho, who is discussed under a different category, but features Corinna, Myrtis, Telesilla, and Praxilla.) This illustrates how quickly and sharply even the most traditional taxonomies are revised if present interests are involved. The history of literary taxonomies might be written, à la Foucault, in terms of repression and of protest against it, of the struggle for power in the competition of discourses and of literary historians.

I come now to taxonomies formed on the basis of what we may call external facts—facts external to the texts themselves. Unlike taxonomies derived from tradition, these presuppose and require positivistic literary scholarship. We may discover, for example, that authors felt affinities with certain of their contemporaries or even viewed and presented themselves as members of a group in manifestoes, journals, joint publications, anthologies, and the like. To classify them together reflects their own self-understanding and, usually, the perceptions of their contemporaries.

As I explain in more detail in the next chapter, it was natural for contemporaries to associate Wordsworth and Coleridge, since they published a joint volume of poems (*Lyrical Ballads*) and introduced it with a preface stating their shared views on poetry; at least they were interpreted as shared views at the time. Moreover, Wordsworth

[14] Sir Philip Sidney, *Miscellaneous Prose*, ed. Katherine Duncan-Jones and Jan Van Dorsten (Oxford: Clarendon, 1973) 83.

and Coleridge were known to be friends, and Coleridge frequently praised Wordsworth's poetry. It was also reasonable to group Robert Southey with them, since Coleridge and Southey were brothers-in-law and shared the same house. Since all three poets lived within twenty miles of each other in the Lake District of England, they were known as the Lake school. These facts and many others, plus the mere effect of grouping them together, caused a presumption that their poems were similar in style, theme, and *Weltanschauung*, and similarities among them were found. The Lake school has interestingly lapsed as a taxonomic term, but Wordsworth and Coleridge are still closely associated in the mind of every reader.

Somewhat similar observations could be made about the Bloomsbury group, the Pre-Raphaelites, the Georgian poets, the Imagists, the association of Eliot with Pound, of Addison with Steele, and many others. Groups of writers may also feel themselves to be united by the influence of the same predecessor or contemporary. The poets of the Auden group in the 1930s are an example, and so are the poets of the Black Mountain school in relation to Pound and the Sons of Ben in relation to Jonson. In all of these cases, the taxonomy has become a part of cultural tradition, but it was grounded at first in affinities that the authors and their contemporaries asserted. Generally we do not know about these contemporary perceptions from reading literary texts but, instead, from ancillary documents, such as letters, manifestoes, and critical essays.

When, in 1960, Donald Allen brought out his anthology *The New American Poetry*, the poets he wished to include were relatively little known. As he said in his preface, the field was "almost completely uncharted."[15] Yet, in presenting his poets, he wished to divide them into groups. Like every thoughtful taxonomer, he knew that his divisions were "somewhat arbitrary," but he

[15] Donald M. Allen, ed., *The New American Poetry* (New York: Grove, 1960) xiv.

thought they were necessary "to give the reader some sense of milieu and to make the anthology more a readable book and less still another collection of 'anthology pieces'" (xii–xiii). In order to classify, he relied mainly on "external facts." He made one group out of those who had published in the same journals, namely, *Origin* and *Black Mountain Review*; several of them had also taught or studied at Black Mountain College.

Geography partly determined other groups: the San Francisco Renaissance, the New York poets. Many of the poets were personally interactive with others in their group. For example, "John Ashbery, Kenneth Koch, and Frank O'Hara, of the fourth group, the New York Poets, first met at Harvard where they were associated with the Poets' Theatre. They migrated to New York in the early fifties where they met Edward Field, Barbara Guest, and James Schuyler, and worked with the Living Theatre and the Artists' Theatre" (xiii).

Possibly another anthologist, selecting a different set of external facts, would have produced a different system of taxonomy. Yet Allen's groupings lasted. We talked for many years of Black Mountain poets, San Francisco poets, and New York poets. To some extent we still do. The fact may testify to some virtue of Allen's classification, but it certainly illustrates the inertia of cultural transmission. Once Allen had constructed his groups, they organized contemporary poetry for other readers and critics. This taxonomy was now a part of cultural tradition, and any retaxonomizing of the same poets would be on the basis Allen had provided.

To classify by observing similarities and differences between texts is very uncommon in literary histories. More exactly, the process is used to confirm classifications that have been obtained in some other way. Observation and comparison of texts are almost never the *sole* basis of a category. One sees why if one considers how vulnerable such procedures are to criticisms of the Crocean type. Since texts have innumerable aspects, they can be linked to innumerable different texts with which they share one or a few aspects, though otherwise the texts thus linked may be quite unlike. If, in other words, we choose only a few aspects as the basis of our classification, address only one or a few questions to literary works (e.g., does it have fourteen lines? does it have a happy ending?), and proceed rigorously, we would make strange collocations, would group texts that we feel, intuitively, do not belong together. And the attempt to classify on the basis of *all* textual aspects would be hopeless. We could not discriminate them in one text or compare them with all the aspects of another text. If we decide to classify by means of a set of significant aspects, we would have to justify our criteria of significance.

Wittgenstein's famous remarks on "family resemblance" are relevant to these dilemmas but do not resolve them.[16] When we align a number of instances under the same concept, the reason is not, Wittgenstein says, because they share an "essence," but because of "a complicated network of similarities overlapping and crisscrossing: sometimes overall similarities, sometimes similarities of detail."[17] Texts are grouped together when they exhibit a number of features that belong to the type, even if they also have anomalous features. But Wittgenstein also says that before we look for family resemblance, we assume there is a family: "Don't look for similarities in order to justify a concept, but also for connections. The father transmits his name to his son even if the latter is quite unlike him."[18] My point is not that Fowler's Wittgen-

---

[16] Wittgenstein's metaphor is adopted by Alastair Fowler in *Kinds of Literature: An Introduction to the Theory of Genres and Modes* (Cambridge: Harvard UP, 1982) 41, to explain the way in which different works in a genre are interrelated.

[17] Ludwig Wittgenstein, *Philosophical Investigations*, trans. G. E. M. Anscombe (Oxford: Basil Blackwell, 1968) 32.

[18] Ludwig Wittgenstein, *Remarks on the Philosophy of Psychology*, ed. G. E. M. Anscombe and G. H. von Wright, trans. G. E. M. Anscombe (Oxford: Basil Blackwell, 1980) 1:923.

steinian theory of genre is mistaken. On the contrary, it makes a large stride forward. But even the concept of family resemblance does not allow us to construct classes or types merely by observing and comparing texts. We must also consider external facts such as filiation.

Yet occasionally a naive literary historian will attempt to construct types and assign texts to them merely by observing similarities, and the attempts illustrate the difficulties. We may cite a passage from Allardyce Nicoll's *British Drama*, where Nicoll classifies some obscure plays written between 1550 and 1575.[19] He begins with dramas in "tragicomic" form, of which there are, he says, three subvarieties. "Moral interludes," the first subtype, include "abstractly named characters," much "farcical-comic business," and the Vice as a central figure. The "second group of plays shows the mixture of the serious and the comic in another way." Though "the plots are for the most part taken from classical sources," the "influence of the morality tradition is apparent." The style is "romantic." And so forth. The third group exploits conventions of chivalric romance. In connection with each subvariety, Nicoll lists examples and discusses one play as a paradigm.

The construction of types is necessary for Nicoll's project, since he lacks space to discuss each play individually and, moreover, wishes to generalize. No one has classified this particular collection of plays before, though Nicoll is, of course, furnished with a fund of concepts, such as morality play and chivalric romance, that he can apply. Armed with these, he observes the plays and tries to determine which ones most resemble which other ones. The typology he makes was not current in the period he is discussing; that is, spectators and readers did not collocate the texts in question under Nicoll's types. Yet Nicoll does not suppose, I imagine, that his divisions are merely conveniences of exposition, as Croce would

[19] Allardyce Nicoll, *British Drama*, 5th ed. (New York: Barnes and Noble, 1963) 61–66.

have maintained, but feels that they are objectively grounded in characteristics of the plays themselves, in differences and resemblances anyone may observe.

Yet it seems clear that other scholars using the same methods would have created different divisions—probably very different ones. To show this, we need only point out that Nicoll's are unconvincing. The three types are not clearly distinguished from each other. The first are moral interludes, and plays in the second group show the influence of the morality tradition. Obviously, many plays might go into either group. The second group is romantic in style; the third exploits the conventions of chivalric romance. The criteria Nicoll uses to taxonomize are of different kinds. Some refer to subject matter (chivalric romance, classical sources), some to types of character (the Vice), some to stage techniques (farcical-comic business). Obviously Nicoll is simply picking out whatever characteristics happen to strike him, and a different reader would be struck by different characteristics. Nicoll's typology is subjective and arbitrary.

The construction of genres by literary historians relies on a combination of observation and positivistic scholarship producing relevant external facts, and it also relies heavily on inference. We may follow Alastair Fowler, for example, as he argues that during the Renaissance the genre of georgic poetry flourished in England.[20] Rosalie Colie maintains that a Renaissance genre evokes a system of values, a "set of interpretations" or "fixes" on the world (8). Referring to Renaissance books on gardening and to the work ethic of the Protestant reformers, Fowler argues that the climate of opinion was favorable to the georgic ethos. He says there was enthusiasm for model poems—Hesiod and Virgil's *Georgics*. He consults the conceptions of the genre in Renaissance critical writings. From all this, he extrapolates "the idea of georgic" around

[20] Alastair Fowler, "The Beginnings of English Georgic," in *Renaissance Genres* 105–25.

1600;[21] in other words, he decides how a reader would have recognized a georgic poem and what expectations that recognition would have activated. He instances many poems that by this idea are georgic or partly georgic, though he does not cite any reader who actually recognized one of them as such.

Thus, in dealing with genres, as with any taxonomy, the literary historian must establish a canon (what texts belong to the genre) and a concept. Both the canon and the concept are more or less uncertain: Fowler says that the Renaissance conception of georgic was "unfocussed" (109). In fact, contemporary genre theory always undermines the unity and coherence of a genre while also asserting it. Contemporary theorists emphasize that genres change over time (Fowler, Cohen), that works incorporate features of several different genres (Bakhtin, Guillen), that there are mixed genres (Colie), and that works in a genre may be linked only by family resemblance (Fowler).

Given these emphases, it seems that very different works may belong to the same genre and that a work may belong to different genres. If this is so, the actual role of genre concepts in the production and reception of works must often be less than genre theorists suppose. Because it depends so heavily on constructions of the literary historian, the description of a genre may be no less creative than the writing of literary history is generally.

In his book *Restoration Tragedy*, Eric Rothstein is inclined to settle his canon by a bold stroke highly characteristic of this scholar. A play is tragedy, he declares, if it says so on the title page. But he at once adds, or if it is "quite similar in form and tone to those that are labeled 'tragedy,'" thus reintroducing the interpretive, constructive process that he wants to avoid.[22] For how does Roth-

---

[21] Fowler, "Beginnings of English Georgic" 111.

[22] Eric Rothstein, *Restoration Tragedy: Form and the Process of Change* (Madison: U of Wisconsin P, 1967) ix.

stein know which features of the plays labeled tragedy
were actually criteria of tragedy and which were irrelevant to this question? To make this judgment, he must
first know the Restoration concept of tragedy. But Rothstein's excellent chapter "Tragic Theory in the Restoration" shows that many and opposing ideas of tragedy were
entertained. He has to compare the ideas, not always self-
consistent, of Rymer, Dryden, Dennis, Filmer, Rowe,
Rapin, and others in order to produce a relatively unified
concept (which, of course, Rothstein requires) that actually belonged to no one in the period.

Pondering at length a closely similar problem in the
Origin of German Tragic Drama, Walter Benjamin decides that positivistic methods of taxonomy lead inevitably to a vortex of skepticism. Classification must proceed
from the "perception of a higher order than is offered by
the point of view of a scholarly verism."[23] He argues that
tragic drama (*Trauerspiel*) is an idea, an original essence,
and as such exists independently of the texts that mani-
fest it. Benjamin recognizes, however, that his resort to
idealist metaphysics is a desperate move. He can see no
other solution.

Of course, a literary classification is usually derived,
not from one procedure, but from several at once. Tradition, present interests, self-classifications of authors,
views of contemporaries, and observed features of texts
may all play a role. In *The Norton Anthology of English
Literature,* Robert Adams says, "One may well think of
the metaphysical poets who followed Donne (Herbert,
Crashaw, Vaughan, Cowley, Cleveland) as trying to draw
out the traditional lyric of love and devotion by stretching it . . . to encompass new unities. . . . In the opposite
direction, Jonson and his 'sons' the Cavalier poets (Carew,
Herrick, Suckling, Waller, Davenant) generally tried to
compress and limit their poems, giving them a high

[23] Walter Benjamin, *Ursprung des deutschen Trauerspiels,* ed. Rolf
Tiedemann (Frankfurt a. M.: Suhrkamp, 1963) 25.

finish."[24] In this typical example, poets are divided into two schools, the poets of each school are listed, and rudimentary concepts of each category are suggested. The taxonomy is traditional, but it is also grounded in affinities the poets asserted. The Cavaliers viewed themselves as Sons of Ben, united by descent from Ben Jonson. And Adams maintains that each group had its own repertoire of thematic and stylistic characteristics.

Finally, taxonomies are also determined by the logical and aesthetic requirements of literary history. In the simplest instances, the literary historian attempts to organize classifications into an elegant system or structure. The types of authors or texts are configured according to logical patterns of simple antithesis, dialectic, part/whole, and so on. Aesthetic considerations are a much more extensive, various, and complicated factor in literary classification than has yet been realized.[25] I have space to consider only one example. In *Fin-de-Siècle Vienna*, Carl Schorske groups together two young Viennese writers, Leopold von Andrian and Hugo von Hofmannsthal. His ostensible reasons for grouping them together are that they were friends, belonged to the same artistic circle, came from the same social class, and shared the same artistic mission.[26]

While he classifies them together, Schorske also ar-

[24] Robert W. Adams, "The Seventeenth Century (1603–1660)," in *The Norton Anthology of English Literature*, ed. M. H. Abrams et al., 4th ed. (New York: Norton, 1979) 1053.

[25] I know only one explicit recognition of the importance of this factor. It comes in a brief, general statement of Francis Berry in "The Present Willed Shortening of Memory," *New Literary History* 2 (Autumn 1970): 58: since the historian "must divide his book into chapters and sections, he will divide his matter into periods. The need for order and balance in the construction of his book, such as a general equality in the length of chapters, might indeed persuade him to present his matter so that it seems to have an order it does not possess. The aesthetic needs of his book may then decide to some extent the division into periods."

[26] Carl Schorske, *Fin-de-Siècle Vienna* (New York: Knopf, 1980) 303–4.

gues—this is an all-important move—that Andrian and
Hofmannsthal are representative. Schorske compares
them (implicitly) with their contemporaries, and asserts
that their family background and shared ideology were
characteristic of their time, place, and generation. They
belonged to what Edward Wechssler calls an *Altersgenos-
senschaft,*[27] and shared, Schorske says, "the values and
spiritual problems of the young generation of the 1890s."

According to Schorske, these authors were aesthetes.
This is, in fact, a traditional characterization of their
work in the 1890s. Once he has the concept (aestheticism) and the texts (writings of Andrian and Hofmannsthal) in mind, Schorske can reason in a hermeneutic
circle. As a literary movement, aestheticism was, Schorske
says, not created in Austria but in France, England, and
Belgium. Moreover, he assumes that his readers are more
familiar with aestheticism in its French or its Pre-
Raphaelite forms. He derives the content of the concept
from accepted exemplars of aestheticism in England,
France, and Belgium, and applies it to the writings of
Andrian and Hofmannsthal. As he goes back and forth
between the foreign concept and the Austrian writings,
he points out discrepancies, and thus he defines an
Austrian aestheticism. (He can generalize from Andrian
and Hofmannsthal to Austrian literary culture because
he has said that they are typical of Austrian writers of
their generation.) The description of Austrian aestheticism was Schorske's goal all along.

Andrian and Hofmannsthal are models of Austrian
aestheticism, it turns out, because this concept was
modeled on them. If Schorske had other Austrian aesthetes of the 1890s, such as Richard Beer-Hofmann or
Felix Dörmann, in mind, his description of Austrian aestheticism would be different. Similarly his description of
English aestheticism is framed in terms of William Mor-

[27] Edward Wechssler, *Die Generation als Jugendreihe und ihr
Kampf um die Denkform* (Leipzig: Quelle and Meyer, 1930).

ris and the Pre-Raphaelites, and if Schorske had Swinburne and Wilde in mind, he could not maintain, as he does, that English aesthetes were engaged in their society. His reasoning is controlled throughout by the examples he has chosen.

It becomes important, therefore, to know why he chose Andrian and Hofmannsthal as his examples, and the reason is a formal one. The theme of Schorske's chapter is the image of the garden in Austrian literature, and in writings of Andrian and Hofmannsthal, this image is more powerful and elaborate than in the works of other Austrian writers of the time. The coherence Schorske seeks to give the chapter dictates his use of Andrian and Hofmannsthal as example, and the examples shape his concept of Austrian aestheticism. Thus Schorske's taxonomy is determined by the aesthetic requirements of his own work.

Literary classifications have generally been constructed by an intuitive synthesis of multiple considerations. Few literary historians have reflected upon the processes by which they obtained their classifications. They have worked naively and ad hoc, often without a distinct consciousness of the basis of their classification, whether it was received opinion, readings of the texts, narrative or aesthetic necessity, their own interests, or a combination of these and others. Almost never have literary historians asked themselves what considerations ought to be the basis of classifications. With rare exceptions, such as Benjamin, they have stopped at vague remarks to the effect that all classifications are unsatisfactory, a truth that does nothing to clarify what might be more acceptable, what less, and by what criteria. Such innocence is no longer possible. Literary historians may continue to classify by the same procedures and reasons as in the past. But they will have to reflect on their moves, and they will have to justify them specifically in their histories.

5

The Construction of English Romantic Poetry as a Literary Classification

THE ENGLISH ROMANTIC MOVEMENT IS A CONstruction of literary historians, and in this chapter I consider the processes by which it was made. I also address the question of why epochal breaks come when they do. Why, in other words, do literary historians generally agree that a new period, named romanticism, begins in English literature around the turn of the nineteenth century. If, as I think, the answer is partly that there is a necessary inertia in these matters—in other words, we continue to perceive epochal breaks in the same places where they have once been seen—the questions then become, who first identified the epochal break that is now accepted? what led them to do so? and why did their contemporaries agree with them?

This chapter also highlights the relation—or gap—between two different moments in the making of classifications. On the one hand, there is the positing of an epochal break or, in the case of a literary movement, the grouping of authors or texts. On the other hand, there is the characterizing of the epoch or group. The latter involves conceptualizing the classification that has been made. A literary historian always pursues these moments simultaneously, reasoning in a hermeneutic circle from a concept to a set of texts and from the set of texts to the concept. But at the level of literary history as an institution, as the collective effort of many literary historians, these moments can separate. There can be consensus in perceiving an epoch or movement long before there is any consensus in characterizing it. In the creation of English romantic poetry as a classification, the grouping of the poets and the development of the concept of romanticism were partly independent processes. Not until the 1890s was the concept of romanticism generally used to interconnect all of the English poets of the early part of the century.

The history of the classification English romantic poetry has been narrated by Wellek in 1949 and by Whalley in much more detail in 1972.[1] Writing when they did, neither Wellek nor Whalley had occasion to emphasize certain aspects of the subject: the self-periodization of the early nineteenth century; the interpretive tradition throughout the century that connected the revolution in poetry to the one in France; the break in this tradition at the end of the nineteenth century, when, for most readers, romanticism first became the name for this movement; the ideological character of the classification; and the significance of it as background to some types of historicist criticism of the romantic poets at present.

As critics have pointed out,[2] fundamental premises of literary history as a discipline come to us from the romantic period. Among these are the importance attached to beginnings or origins, the assumption that a development is the subject of literary history, the understanding of development as continual rather than disjunctive, and the creation of suprapersonal entities as the subjects of this development. Therefore, if we were to trace the origin and development of these premises, we would be writ-

[1] René Wellek, "The Concept of Romanticism in Literary History," in *Concepts of Criticism*, ed. Stephen G. Nichols, Jr. (New Haven: Yale UP, 1963) 128–98; George Whalley, "England: Romantic-Romanticism," in *"Romantic" and Its Cognates*, ed. Hans Eichner (Toronto: U of Toronto P, 1972) 157–62.

[2] Clifford Siskin, *The Historicity of Romantic Discourse* (New York: Oxford UP, 1988); Cynthia Chase in conversation.

ing a romantic type of literary history, though at a higher level of reflection. A narrative history of the classification of English romantic poetry may also be a romantic project. To the narrative I am about to tell, there is, however, a more telling objection. Since I argue in chapter 2 that narrative literary history cannot represent the past, it is self-contradictory to make the attempt. We shall have to ponder the justification of this narrative after it has been made.

Classificatory constructions, such as movements, genres, traditions, and periods, have three parts: a name, a concept or characterization (what romanticism is), and a canon of writers or set of texts included in the classification. I shall scarcely deal with the changing canon and concept, but shall ask how and why very diverse writers were amalgamated into a movement and how this movement was named *romantic*.[3]

Some familiar points must be noted. In England between 1798 and 1824, the term *romantic* did not designate a contemporary literary movement or period. The adjective was widely current, and meant wonderful, exotic, like a medieval romance. After 1813, the influential distinction of the Schlegel brothers between classical literature or culture and the romantic or modern was known to English critics, but in this distinction *romantic* or *modern* referred to the literature of the late Middle Ages and Renaissance.[4] The poets we now group together seemed very different. On the whole, they disliked each

[3] Recent history of this classification, with reference to disputes over periodization since 1940, is surveyed by Mark Parker, "Measure and Countermeasure: The Lovejoy-Wellek Debate and Romantic Periodization," in *Theoretical Issues in Literary History*, ed. David Perkins (Cambridge: Harvard UP, 1991) 227–47.

[4] The Schlegels' seminal comparison of the ancient or classical and the romantic or modern was known to Crabb Robinson by 1803, to Coleridge by 1812, and to a great many other persons after Madame de Staël's *Germany* and A. W. Schlegel's *Course of Lectures on Dramatic Art* were published in English translations in 1813 and 1815, respectively. See Herbert Weisinger, "English Treatment of the Classical-Romantic Prob-

other at least as much as they were friendly and admiring. To the poets and their contemporaries, their relative standing at present would have seemed time's incomprehensible caprice. The canon of contemporary poets in 1820 generally began with Byron, Scott, Campbell, Wordsworth, and Moore. Blake was unknown; Shelley and Keats had few readers; the genius of Coleridge as a poet was not widely recognized.

There were taxonomies, of course. Reviewing Southey's *Thalaba, the Destroyer* in 1802, Francis Jeffrey grouped Wordsworth, Coleridge, Southey, and Lamb together as a *"sect* of poets."[5] References to this school gradually became common in the literature of the time, and by 1814 Wordsworth, Coleridge, and Southey were familiarly known as the Lake poets.[6] In 1817, in a move frankly modeled on Jeffrey's, John Gibson Lockhart invented the Cockney school of poetry, writing a series of notoriously abusive articles in *Blackwood's Edinburgh Magazine.* This school had Leigh Hunt for its chief and included Keats and John Hamilton Reynolds; according to John Wilson, Hazlitt was the cockney mouthpiece.[7] In Lockhart's lexicon, cockney implied low birth, poor education, bad taste, vulgarity, and affectation—an ill-bred aping of the tastes and manners of superiors. This snobbish classification was motivated, as Lockhart frankly says, by ideological hostility. The conservative Lockhart wrote to annihilate the radical Leigh Hunt, and was perhaps the more inflamed at a time when riots and conspiracies among workers and the government's use of agents provocateurs had newly fanned political passions. (Lockhart also had commercial motivations for journalistic violence, since he and John Wilson had just been hired to revive *Black-*

lem," *MLQ* 7 (1946): 477–88; Wellek, *Concepts of Criticism* 145–47; Whalley 199–216.

   [5] Francis Jeffrey, *Edinburgh Review* 1 (Oct. 1802): 64.

   [6] John Taylor Coleridge, *Quarterly Review* 11 (Apr. 1814): 178.

   [7] John Wilson, *Blackwood's Edinburgh Magazine* 13 (Apr. 1823): 457.

wood's Edinburgh Magazine.) The Cockney school was occasionally repeated as a taunt, especially by reviewers in *Blackwood's*, but, unlike the Lake school, it was never taken seriously as a literary classification. The same may be said of Southey's invention, in the preface to his *The Vision of Judgment* (1821), of the satanic school of poets. Readers understood that this was merely another episode in the long enmity of Southey and Byron.

Since the Lake school was accepted as a meaningful classification and had a long career in literary history, we may look further into its creation. It derives, as I said, from one influential critic, Francis Jeffrey.[8] In making this classification, Jeffrey was guided by bibliographical and biographical information. Coleridge had inserted lines of his own in Southey's *Joan of Arc*; the second edition of Coleridge's *Poems* (1797) included lyrics by Charles Lamb and Charles Lloyd; the *Lyrical Ballads* (1798) was a joint publication of Wordsworth and Coleridge; Coleridge, Southey, and their families shared a house in Keswick, and Coleridge frequently visited Wordsworth in Grasmere. Knowing that they were personally associated, Jeffrey found similarities of "style and manner" in their poetry: simplicity of form and language, love of nature, longing for the ideal, and "paradoxical morality."[9] Jeffrey read the preface to the second edition of the *Lyrical Ballads* as the program for a new poetry.

Among Jeffrey's motives in making this classification, an ideological one was prominent. This "sect of poets," he said, "are *dissenters* from the established systems in poetry and criticism. . . . A splenetic and idle discontent

---

[8] But Jeffrey's classification was vaguely anticipated by an anonymous reviewer in the *Monthly Mirror* 11 (June 1801): 389: "The new school of philosophy . . . has introduced a new school of poetry." It is not clear which poets the reviewer had in mind, but he finds in their poems "a romantic search after simplicity."

[9] *Edinburgh Review* 1 (Oct. 1802): 64. See Jeffrey's subsequent account of his reasons for classifying these poets together in *Edinburgh Review* 28 (Aug. 1817): 509.

with the existing institutions of society, seems to be at the bottom of all their serious and peculiar sentiments."[10] To compare them to Dissenters was not yet to call them revolutionaries, but the Dissenters lived under political and social disabilities and were frequently associated with radical causes and agitation. In politics, Jeffrey was a moderate Whig, a gradualist, who wanted reform but not sudden and drastic change that would tear the social fabric. In 1802, bread shortages were intensifying popular unrest. The poor might be supposed to be seditious and so might writers who sympathized with the poor.

In 1802, the French Revolution naturally magnetized Jeffrey's thoughts and emotions; in fact, he referred to it in the same issue of the *Edinburgh Review* (63). In the "discontent" of these poets, who had borrowed some of their "leading principles . . . from the great apostle of Geneva," Jeffrey sensed a state of mind akin to that of the *philosophes*, the French intellectuals whose writings had contributed to the Revolution. Doctrinaire and subversive, the poets were the more dangerous if they were a sect, a group, a potential party. Fear of revolution, in other words, did not influence merely Jeffrey's characterization of them; it also prompted him to see them as a group.

Later, Jeffrey made the analogy to the revolutionists more clearly, as though he became gradually more conscious of it and more alarmed. In 1805, he reviewed Southey's *Madoc* and took the occasion to comment on "the ambition of Mr. Southey and some of his associates." Their ambition was not "of that regulated and manageable sort which usually grows up in old established commonwealths" but was "of a more undisciplined and revolutionary character," which "looks, we think, with a jealous and contemptuous eye on the old aristocracy of the literary world."[11]

[10] *Edinburgh Review* 1 (Oct. 1802): 71.
[11] *Edinburgh Review* 7 (Oct. 1805): 1.

The Lake school, then, was a classification created by one critic. External facts suggested to Jeffrey that there was a group and gave him the canon of poets to be included in it; with these in mind, he perceived similarities of style and manner in the poets' texts. In his 1802 review of Southey, he reasoned in a hermeneutic circle, going to and fro between his concepts of the group and their texts. Ideological factors motivated his perception that there was a group and determined his hostility to it and his characterization of it. The classification caught on because of Jeffrey's prestige as a critic, because it satisfied the need readers always feel to organize the contemporary literary scene, and because much evidence seemed to confirm it. Once a classification has established itself in the minds of readers, it may continue to be used while the characterization of it changes enormously. By 1814, the Lake school was a generally accepted classification and no longer necessarily hostile. It had a long life in literary history and finally died as a classification into the more comprehensive one of romanticism—the romantic movement.[12]

But the Lake school included only a few of the writers we now group together as romantic. A ground was created in England in the 1810s for the later move that united almost all writers of the age in one classification. We do not derive our concept of periods directly from the romantics, but from Dilthey by way of German *Geistesgeschichte* around the turn of this century. But the romantics entertained the concept of a literary/cultural period as we now possess it—or possessed it until recently, since periodization is currently under searching question. This concept is, as Teesing puts it, of a "tract of time that is relatively unified and different from others in a characteristic way"; "a time section," to quote Wellek

---

[12] Whalley (220–30) narrates the history of the critical construction of the Lake school.

again, "dominated by a system of literary norms, standards, and conventions."[13]

No one has put better than Shelley the concept of a period as a *Wirkungszusammenhang*, to use Dilthey's word, as a complex of interrelated effects: "There must be a resemblance," says Shelley, "which does not depend on their own will between all the writers of any particular age. They cannot escape from subjection to a common influence which arises out of an infinite combination of circumstances belonging to the times in which they live, though each is in a degree the author of the very influence by which his being is pervaded."[14]

In the histories of English poetry planned first by Pope and then by Gray, though written by neither, the divisions of the material would not have been by periods but by "schools," a taxonomic category borrowed from discussions of painting. Pope would have noticed the school of Spenser, the school of Donne, and so forth, and in a letter to Warton, Gray, who had a copy of Pope's plan, set forth a similar one of his own. After the poetry of the Celts and of the Goths, which is characterized by racial qualities, Gray perceived a succession of schools: the school of Provence (Chaucer to Dunbar), the second Italian school (Surrey, Wyatt, et al.), and the school of Spenser, which "ends in Milton." Eighteenth-century poetry belonged to the "School of France introduced after the Restoration . . . which has continued down to our own times."[15]

The romantic concept of period inherited the histori-

---

[13] H. P. H. Teesing, *Das Problem der Perioden in der Literaturgeschichte* (Groningen: J. B. Wolters, 1949) 8; René Wellek and Austin Warren, *Theory of Literature* (New York: Harcourt, Brace, 1949) 277.

[14] P. B. Shelley, Preface to "The Revolt of Islam," in *Selected Poems, Essays, and Letters*, ed. Ellsworth Barnard (New York: Odyssey, 1944) 524; cf. preface to "Prometheus Unbound," 95: "Poets, not otherwise than philosophers, painters, sculptors, and musicians, are, in one sense, the creators, and, in another, the creations, of their age. From this subjection the loftiest do not escape."

[15] Thomas Gray, *Correspondence*, ed. Paget Toynbee et al. (Oxford: Clarendon, 1935) 3:1123–24. For further discussion of these projects see

cal sophistication and relativism that had been growing
in England over the last hundred years.[16] Gradually, but
with massive effect, similar ideas were received from Germany, especially from Herder and the Schlegels. It might
seem that a strong interest in periodization necessarily
presupposes a commitment to historical relativism. But
intellectuals in England were not yet thoroughgoing historical relativists, as is illustrated in the brief literary histories offered by Jeffrey and Shelley.[17] Both share the
enthusiastic rhetoric and newer tastes of their times —
Jeffrey in his ardor for the Elizabethans and Shelley for
Petrarch and Dante also. But both adhere to the traditional assumption that the norms of poetic excellence are
universal and unchanging. Hence, their histories of poetry
are of declines and revivals, of the footsteps of poetry recur-
rently departing from the world and returning. They did
not assume, as the Schlegels already did, that the poetry of
different times and places is incommensurable, embody-
ing completely different but equally valid ideals, and that
the poetry of each period is to be appreciated from within
its own system of values. In romantic England,
the interest in self-periodization — in recognizing their
time as a period and in characterizing its unity — was not
stimulated primarily by relativistic premises. There was a
more specific and immediate factor.

In the early nineteenth century there were many discussions of "the spirit of the age." Some of these are noted
by Wellek in "The Concept of Romanticism," others by
M. H. Abrams in "English Romanticism: The Spirit of
the Age," and more recently by Abrams in "Revolutionary Romanticism 1790–1990: Introduction."[18] Whether

Reneé Wellek, *The Rise of English Literary History* (Chapel Hill: U of
North Carolina P, 1941) 162–65.

[16] See Wellek 52–53, 58–65, 103, 139, 162–65.

[17] Francis Jeffrey, *Edinburgh Review* 18 (Aug. 1811):275–84; P. B.
Shelley, "A Defence of Poetry," in *Selected Poems* 541–56.

[18] Wellek, *Concepts of Criticism* 152–56; M. H. Abrams, "English
Romanticism: The Spirit of the Age," in *The Correspondent Breeze:*

such passages refer only to the poetry of the age or to the age in general, they all testify to a sense that the times were new, unified, and different from any past epoch.

For the sense that their own age was a period, the overwhelming reason was, as Abrams says, the French Revolution or, more exactly, the extent to which this event preoccupied thought and emotion.[19] It made a break in historical continuity. If one did not feel this oneself, one was persuaded by Edmund Burke, who was able, as has been said, to "sway the intelligent as a demogogue sways a mob." There had been, Burke emphasizes, nothing like it in the past. The Revolution opened a new epoch of history. And whether one favored or abhorred the Revolution, a great many other events or manifestations in contemporary social and cultural life could be, and were, related to it by contemporary interpreters. The Revolution was, in their eyes, a universal cause, a factor in most of the powerful tendencies of the time, a ground of the unity of their age.

Whatever the political allegiance of the essayist, the spirit of the age was always described as impatient of authority and limits, and this spirit was said also to animate literature. Other determinants of the age such as, in Jeffrey's analysis, "the rise or revival of a general spirit of methodism in the lower orders" and the extent "of our political and commercial relations, which have . . . familiarized all ranks of people with distant countries, and great undertakings," reinforced the "agitations of the

Essays on English Romanticism (New York: W. W. Norton, 1984) 44–46; M. H. Abrams, "Revolutionary Romanticism 1790–1990: Introduction," *Bucknell Review*, forthcoming. For additional remarks of a similar kind see the *Critical Review* 5, 4th ser. (Feb. 1814): 144; Francis Jeffrey, *Edinburgh Review* 23 (Apr. 1814): 200–201; Leigh Hunt, Preface to *Foliage, or, Poems Original and Translated,* in *Leigh Hunt's Literary Criticism,* ed. L. H. and C. W. Houtchens (New York: Columbia UP, 1956) 129–30; John Wilson, *Blackwood's Edinburgh Magazine* 7 (May 1820): 206; *General Weekly Register* (30 June 1822): 501–2.

    [19] *Correspondent Breeze* 44–47; "Revolutionary Romanticism."

French Revolution" and contributed to the same tendencies. All these factors, including the "impression of the new literature of Germany," worked together to create "an effectual demand for more profound speculation, and more serious emotion than was dealt in by writers of the former century."[20] "The last half-century has produced," said the *Critical Review*, "as great a revolution in the world of fiction as of fact. Within that time established customs have been set aside, grave opinions derided, and the bounds of poetic license extended beyond the limits of ordinary vision. Lord Byron is one of the mighty spirits who lead the revolt."[21] For a final statement, we can turn again to Jeffrey in 1814:

> This is the stage of society in which fanaticism has its second birth, and political enthusiasm its first true development—when plans of visionary reform, and schemes of boundless ambition are conceived . . . the era of revolutions and projects—of vast performances, and infinite expectations. Poetry . . . becomes more enthusiastic, authoritative and impassioned; and feeling the necessity of dealing in more powerful emotions than suited the tranquil and frivolous age which preceded, naturally goes back to those themes and characters which animated the energetic lays of its first rude inventors. . . . This is the age to which we are now arrived.[22]

Metaphors control perceptions, and the spirit of the age must obviously unite all writers of the time, however different they may seem. So far as I know, this point was first made explicitly with reference to the contemporary poets by John Wilson in 1820: "The age has unquestionably produced a noble band of British Poets—each separated from all the rest by abundant peculiarities of style and manner . . . [but] all of them bound together . . . by rich participation in the stirring and exalting spirit of the

---

[20] Francis Jeffrey, *Edinburgh Review* 27 (Sept. 1816): 8.
[21] *Critical Review* 5, 4th ser. (Feb. 1814): 144.
[22] Francis Jeffrey, *Edinburgh Review* 23 (Apr. 1814): 200–201.

same eventful age . . . all kindred to each other by their part in the common Soul and Thought of the time."[23] Here the grouping of the poets is already accomplished, though the classification still has no name and hardly any characterization attached to it.

Wilson's canon is Scott, Byron, Wordsworth, Southey, and Coleridge. The first person to describe the new movement with anything like the canon that prevailed until recently was Leigh Hunt in an 1816 article, on "Young Poets," in *The Examiner*. Observing that "there has been a new school of poetry rising of late, which promises to extinguish the French one that has prevailed among us since the time of Charles the 2nd.," Hunt indicates that the established members of the school are Wordsworth, Southey, Coleridge, and Byron, and that the young poets, Shelley, Keats, and John Hamilton Reynolds, "promise a considerable addition of strength to the new school."[24] Hunt's intention, of course, was to boost the reputations of Shelley, Keats, and Reynolds, with whom he was friendly and politically allied. Ideology influenced his canon as much as it did Wilson's more conservative one.

An ironical result of this periodization, as it first developed, was that, though by the 1810s, Wordsworth, Coleridge, and Southey had long been politically conservative, and Scott had never been anything else, there was a tendency to cast them all in the role of revolutionaries, because of their participation in the spirit of the age.

The first person[25] to name this new school romantic was Taine in 1863, who had a section called "The Romantic School" in his *History of English Literature*. Taine may simply have extended the by then familiar notion of the Lake school to cover all the writers of the period, for he quotes Jeffrey's 1802 article on the "sect" of "dissenters

---

[23] John Wilson, *Blackwood's Edinburgh Magazine* 7 (May 1820): 206.
[24] Leigh Hunt, "Young Poets," *Examiner* (1 Dec. 1816): 761.
[25] I omit the Austrian police spy, cited by Wellek (*Concepts of Criticism* 148), who "reported that Byron belongs to the *Romantici* and 'has written and continues to write poetry of this new school.'"

in poetry," and as he begins to characterize the romantic school, his generalizations apply particularly to Wordsworth, Coleridge, and Southey. Or Taine may have been influenced by the idea of the spirit of the age. But mainly he was constructing the English romantic school on the model of the French, which had already been recognized as a classification: "Now appeared the English romantic school, closely resembling the French."[26]

Taine's description of this school pertains as much to German and French romanticism as to British. He emphasizes, for example, historical relativism as a romantic concept and the extent to which philosophy enters literature. He hardly mentions the romantic orientation to nature until he discusses Shelley. The specifically English quality of the school is its intellectual timidity; its range of speculation is limited by moral and religious commitments. Taine's history was not translated into English until 1871 and had, at first, little impact.

The major Victorian critics — Masson, Arnold, Swinburne, Bagehot, Morley, Stephen, Pater — did not refer to an English romantic movement, though they wrote abundantly about the poets. Neither did the literary historians, Margaret Oliphant (1882), Saintsbury (1896), and Garnett and Gosse (1903–4), though they all use *romantic* as an adjective for this or that tendency or effect in the literature.[27] To refer to the writers collectively, they tended to use the familiar terms *school* or *age*, speaking of the Lake school, the age of Wordsworth, and so forth; the concept of "the age of . . . " seems to hover between

[26] Hippolyte Taine, *History of English Literature* (New York: Frederick Ungar, 1965) 3:422.

[27] Margaret Oliphant, *Literary History of England between the End of the Eighteenth and the Beginning of the Nineteenth Centuries*, 3 vols. (London: Macmillan, 1882); George Saintsbury, *A History of Nineteenth Century Literature (1780–1895)* (London: Macmillan, 1896); Richard Garnett and Edmund Gosse, *English Literature: An Illustrated Record*, vol. 4, *From the Age of Johnson to the Age of Tennyson* (London: William Heinemann, 1903).

that of a period and that of a school headed by a famous artist. In Pater's *Appreciations* (1889), the postscript, which was first published as "Romanticism" in 1876, notes that in Germany and France the term *romantic* "has been used to describe a particular school of writers . . . at a particular period," the implication being that the term was not used this way in England.[28]

On the other hand, David Moir speaks in 1852 of the "purely romantic school" of Scott, Coleridge, Southey, and Hogg, and there is a similarly nebulous reference in Rushton in 1863 and in the work of Shaw as revised by Smith in 1864. In 1873, Dewey refers to the "Romantic School" of Byron, Scott, and Moore; and G. M. Hopkins, in an 1881 letter to Dixon, refers to the "Romantic school" of Keats, Hunt, Hood, and Scott.[29] These are vague, brief remarks, and for none of these critics does the romantic school include all of the major poets in the first decades of the century. But in 1885, in *The Liberal Movement in English Literature*, which first appeared as a series of essays in the *National Review*, W. J. Courthope says, "I might, indeed, have called the series 'The Romantic Movement in English Literature.'"[30] To explain why this would have been a possible title, Courthope refers to

[28] Walter Pater, *Appreciations* (London: Macmillan, 1910) 243.

[29] David Macbeth Moir, *Sketches of the Poetical Literature of the Past Half Century* (Edinburgh: William Blackwood, 1851) 17; William Rushton, "The Classical and Romantic Schools of English Literature: As Represented by Spenser, Dryden, Pope, Scott, and Wordsworth," in *The Afternoon Lectures on English Literature* (London: 1863); Thomas Budd Shaw, *New History of English Literature*, rev. Truman J. Backus (New York: Sheldon, 1878); this is a revision of Shaw's *Outlines of English Literature*, rev. William Smith (London: John Murray, 1864); J. Dewey, *A Comparative Estimate of Modern English Poets* (1873), cited in Samuel C. Chew, *Byron in England: His Fame and After-Fame* (London: John Murray, 1924) 292; Claude Colleer Abbot, ed., *The Correspondence of Gerard Manley Hopkins and Richard Watson Dixon*, rev. ed. (London: Oxford UP, 1955) 98.

[30] William John Courthope, *The Liberal Movement in English Literature* (London: John Murray, 1885) viii.

the now familiar distinction, inherited from the Schlegels, of the classical from the late medieval or romantic and argues that both "streams of inspiration" are united in Chaucer and continue as latent tendencies through the history of English literature. There was a "romantic outburst" in the "early part of the present century."

The reason Courthope entitled his book *The Liberal Movement* is, therefore, revealing. He wishes to highlight the political ethos of romanticism, for he sees political events, emotions, and ideas as its primary historical causes. In other words, he still views what we call romanticism as "the writings of those who, in point of time, followed the French Revolution, and who founded their matter and style on the principles to which that Revolution gave birth." Courthope does not approve of this "movement on behalf of liberty"; he writes as a conservative, and his argument anticipates that of Irving Babbitt. "Liberal," to him, means individual self-expression, desire to reconstruct society according to an ideal, and belief in "unlimited progress." "The spirit of the age embodies itself in the philosophic isolation of Wordsworth; in the rebellion of Byron against society; in the Utopianism of Shelley" (53, 22, xi, 161, 224).

My point is that Courthope, though a spokesman for the conservatism in English intellectual life toward the end of the nineteenth century, was still interpreting the movement at the start of the century as it had been interpreted for sixty years, as a group of writers who were "united by a common spirit," rebellious, libertarian, and expansive (198). Seventeen years earlier, J. C. Shairp said that to refer the "poetic genius" of the early part of the century to the "French Revolution, or to the causes of that Revolution" is one of "the literary commonplaces."[31] Victorian critics used conservatives such as Scott and Coleridge and radicals such as Shelley to voice their own ideologies in

---

[31] J. C. Shairp, *Studies in Poetry and Philosophy* (Edinburgh: David Douglas, 1886) 1. The essay quoted was originally published in 1868.

their commentaries. But until the last decade of the century, the movement was almost always seen as essentially liberal, radical, or revolutionary, whatever may have been the politics of the individual poets. Later views of romanticism as politically multiple in its allegiances or as proto-Fascist mark a massive break with this interpretive tradition, and so do present perceptions of romantic poetry as ideological in a quasi-Marxist sense, as consciously or unconsciously supporting the political status quo. The sixth volume (1910) of Courthope's subsequent *History of English Poetry* is entitled *The Romantic Movement in English Poetry: Effects of the French Revolution.* It was around the turn of this century that the break in interpretive tradition took place, and it coincides with the bestowing of the name *romanticism*.[32]

This renaming had causes and consequences too extensive to be analyzed in a brief chapter, but several factors may be mentioned. For the full understanding of them we must keep in mind the ethos of academic life in those days, for in Great Britain and the United States the school or spirit in question became romantic in the hands of professors. They were of course familiar with the classic/romantic distinction that had been discussed repeatedly throughout the nineteenth century, and it was easy to conflate this with the dichotomy of the French or Augustan school versus the school that had emerged in the later eighteenth century. They were respectful of continental, especially German, scholarship on their subject, and much of this, though not all, referred to a romantic school in England.

Probably, like many professors of English, they were provincial in their knowledge of contemporary tendencies in the literary world but much influenced by the lat-

---

[32] Wellek, *Concepts of Criticism* 150, says the term *romanticism* was "fully established" for English literature at the end of the century "in books such as those of W. L. Phelps and Henry A. Beers"; see also Whalley 157, 160.

est ones of which they were aware. The Pre-Raphaelite view of the romantic poets had an especially large impact on their own conceptions. This was summed up in Theodore Watts-Dunton's essay on "The Renascence of Wonder." This essay was not put together and published until 1904, but the ideas in it were implicit in other essays by Watts-Dunton dating from 1880. Watts-Dunton made the astounding claim that the "Romantic Revival" was not the effect but the cause of the French Revolution. It had this tremendous result because it altered consciousness by reawakening imagination. But Watts-Dunton did not dwell on this claim. He tended, instead, to sever the relations between the English romantic movement and political events by dwelling on the craftsmanship of the poets and on wonder as their primary poetic impulse; by *wonder* he meant, in short, medievalism. Pater also contributed mightily to the depoliticizing and aestheticizing of perceptions of this poetry, as one sees in his famous definition of romanticism as "the addition of strangeness to beauty" (246).

As a further consideration, there is the simple but important fact that professors in those days were committed by the standards of their discipline to positive fact, detail, and qualification. About these diverse poets they found it difficult to make any generalizations, and the political complexion of the movement as a whole seemed a remarkably complicated question.

From the joint working of these factors emerged such books as those by C. H. Herford of Manchester University, C. E. Vaughan of the University of Newcastle-on-Tyne, Henry A. Beers and his student William Lyon Phelps, both of them professors at Yale, and Lewis E. Gates of Harvard.[33] The two books of Beers, still valuable

---

[33] C. H. Herford, *The Age of Wordsworth* (London: George Bell, 1897); C. E. Vaughan, *The Romantic Revolt* (Edinburgh: William Blackwood, 1900); Henry A. Beers, *A History of English Romanticism in the Eighteenth Century* (New York: Henry Holt, 1898) and *A History of English Romanticism in the Nineteenth Century* (New York: Henry

for their encyclopedic thoroughness, are entitled *A History of English Romanticism* but are devoted entirely to the medieval revival; and so, for the most part, is Phelps's book, which deals solely with eighteenth-century authors. (Phelps wrote his book, Beers implies, on the basis of Beers's lectures.)

Herford explains that "almost everything of importance" in the literature of Wordsworth's time "stood in some relation," not to the French Revolution, as would earlier have been claimed, but to "the far-reaching and many-sided revival of imaginative power commonly known as Romanticism," and "Romanticism is thus the organizing conception of the present volume." Its politics fluctuated "from revolution to reaction," but above all it was escapist. Romanticism, for Herford, was "an extraordinary development of imaginative sensibility" to nature, childhood, peasant life, the Middle Ages, ancient Greece, myth, wonder, and romance—all "strange; ways of escape from the ordinary" (vii, xx, xiv).

As for Vaughan, who discusses English literature and the literature of the Continent, the revolt of which he speaks in his title has nothing to do with politics but is against the cramping ethos of the Enlightenment and is in favor of passion, nature, and mystery. Gates takes the same line, arguing that "the Romantic Movement" reasserts "the primacy of the spirit," and that "under this formula may be brought whatever is most characteristic" in all the writers of the age (18). In such works the connection the last century had made between literary and political revolution was quite broken.

But two books published at the same time provided an academic culmination to the interpretive tradition of the nineteenth century: Edward Dowden's *The French Revolution and English Literature* (1897) and, in the United

---

Holt, 1901); William Lyon Phelps, *The Beginnings of the English Romantic Movement* (Boston: Ginn, 1893); Lewis E. Gates, *Studies and Appreciations* (New York: Macmillan, 1900).

States, Albert Elmer Hancock's *The French Revolution and the English Poets* (1899). Both authors grounded in the French Revolution the unity of English poetry in the early part of the century but stressed that the poets responded to it in quite different ways. They deployed the Revolution to explain both the conservatism of Coleridge and the radicalism of Shelley.

In making so much of the French Revolution as a causal factor, Dowden and Hancock were belated. The trend was elsewhere, and the relatively depoliticized romanticism was to flourish for a while in interpretations, so much so that Dowden, Hancock, and the tradition to which they belonged were often forgotten. When Abrams, in the well-known 1963 essay cited earlier, traced the connection between "the political, intellectual, and emotional circumstances of a period of revolutionary upheaval" and "the scope, subject-matter, themes, values and even language of a number of Romantic poems," he emphasized predecessors of his argument (especially Hazlitt) in the romantic period but did not mention that the argument was a commonplace of Victorian criticism. He knew this, of course, but doubtless felt that it would not impress the contemporary critics he wished to correct, who "usually ignore" the relations of the English romantic movement "to the revolutionary climate of the time" (46).

Dowden and Hancock assumed that there was a romantic movement but despaired of defining it. "There are," says Hancock, "no principles comprehensive and common to all [the poets] except those of individualism and revolt"; the "revolt" in question was not political but against the "literary standards" of the eighteenth century.[34] This reluctance to define the unity of a romanticism that the classification posited was typical of professors at the time, the natural result of caution plus erudition. A. O. Lovejoy's famous 1924 essay "On the

---

[34] Albert Elmer Hancock, *The French Revolution and the English Poets* (New York: Henry Holt, 1899) 46–47.

Discrimination of Romanticisms" was in a tradition of perplexity that goes back to the first adoption of the totalizing classification in England and the United States.

Thus, the romantic movement was subjected to deconstructive impulses from the moment it was constructed. Its political thrust was neutralized in the same moment by Pre-Raphaelite trends in criticism, by the continental point of v: ?w of its interpreters, by the effects of positivist scholarshi), and doubtless also by the ideology of English professors. The "romantic ideology" was formed at this time and not in the romantic period itself. The phrase refers, of course, to Jerome McGann's influential analysis of the doctrine that both the subject matter and the style of poetry are "ideal," that "poetry works at the level of final Ideas," that "one may escape such a world [historical reality] through imagination and poetry."[35]

McGann views this doctrine as "ideological" in the Marxist sense of "false consciousness," and attributes this ideology both to the romantic poets and to their critics, especially the New Critics. But though such ideas about poetry are expressed by the romantic poets, along with many contradictory ones, the poetry was usually read, throughout the nineteenth century, as strongly involved in historical reality—and divorced from it only at the end of the nineteenth century.

In his *Theory of the Avant-Garde*, Peter Bürger points out that the political impact of a poem depends not only on its contents but also on "the way art functions in society." The latter is determined by the "institution of art," which includes the economic and social processes governing art's production and distribution and also the assumptions with which it is read. The "institution of art" changes over time and also differs within social groups. According to Bürger, in nineteenth-century bourgeois society, art has the function of neutralizing social criti-

[35] Jerome McGann, *The Romantic Ideology: A Critical Investigation* (Chicago: U of Chicago P, 1983) 101, 131.

cism. All those values, such as "humanity, joy, truth, and solidarity," that could not be "satisfied in everyday life because the principle of competition pervaded all spheres, can find a home in art." There, however, they are confined to "an ideal sphere." By "realizing the image of a better order in fiction, which is semblance (*Schein*) only, [art] relieves the existing society of the pressure of those forces that make for change."[36]

Yet, until the end of the nineteenth century, criticism of the romantic poets suggests a different institution of art. For Victorian critics used the poets to support their own political and ideological commitments. Their perceptions of Wordsworth, Byron, Shelley, and so forth embody the political controversies of the Victorian world. Moreover, the Victorian critics assumed that romantic poetry was similarly engaged in the political life of its time. Only toward the end of the nineteenth century does criticism of this poetry begin to reflect what Bürger calls "aesthetic ideology," in the same moment in which the poetry was classified as romantic.

This development was entirely compatible with the pursuit of *Geistesgeschichte*, and by the joint working of aesthetic ideology and *Geistesgeschichte*, romantic poetry was provided with a new context in the past and a new derivation. Romantic poems were no longer related to the French Revolution but, instead, to intellectual and cultural trends in the eighteenth century—the interest in the primitive, in genius, in the psychology of the imagination, the medieval revival, comparative mythology, sentimentalism, sensationalism, and associationism. Jerome McGann, David Simpson, Alan Liu, and others are now reacting against this interpretation of romantic poetry with a new historicist contextualism.

---

[36] Peter Bürger, *Theory of the Avant-Garde,* trans. Michael Shaw and Jochen Schulte-Sasse (Minneapolis: U of Minnesota P, 1984) 49–50.

Since this chapter has presented a narrative literary history, it is necessary, in a book of this kind, to reflect critically on this construction. If it tells a true story, it does not support the argument of this book, for the argument is that a true story cannot be told. Confronting the strong reasons for such skepticism, many historians and literary historians have retreated to perspectivism as their last stand. Different portraits of the same past may all be accurate, they argue, if the portraits are drawn from different points of view. Or, changing the figure, one might say that each historian follows his own itinerary through the field; the questions asked determine which events are noticed, but the field remains the same. Or, the past is a structure of events, but each historian slices through it at a different angle. Though historians tell different stories about the same past, the stories are compatible. Where there is disagreement, further discussion or research will resolve it. However, I question whether any literary history can be credible, even one that is conceived as perspectival.

The narrative just constructed describes three periods—that of the initial grouping of the poets, that of Victorian criticism of them, and that of the end of the century, when English romantic poetry finally became a totalizing classification. Within these periods, some heterogeneity is exhibited, but, on the whole, the narrative constructs periods much more than it deconstructs them. Thus the narrative fails by the criteria of postmodern or poststructuralist historiography. Yet the periods are necessary for rhetorical and narrative purposes. They demarcate the amorphous into phases and provide clear oppositions and turns of plot.

As it presents the concept of the spirit of the age, the narrative does not challenge the romantic critics who advanced this concept. They said that the age had a spirit, that this was unified, and that its character was determined by the French Revolution. M. H. Abrams positively endorses these ideas in his famous article on the subject. In fact, the cultural manifestations of early nineteenth-century England were no more unified than they ever are. The question then becomes, why did critics at this time so strongly posit the spiritual unity of their age? Ideological functions may have been served. The real social disharmonies and rampant individualism of the age could be overcome at the level of the spirit.

This point is underscored if we contrast the critical interpretations that are made of our own age. We live in a new, postmodernist era, according to many critics, but its character, causes, and cultural worth vary *toto caelo* as one goes from one description of it to the next.[37] Yet, in contrast to the romantic commentators on their own age, our critics generally claim that postmodernism is radically heterogeneous and, moreover, that postmodern man is exceptionally attuned to difference or heterogeneity. In the last clause, I am drawing on Alan Liu's analysis of poststructuralist cultural criticism as detailism. We

[37] John Barth, "The Literature of Exhaustion," *Atlantic Monthly* 220 (Aug. 1967): 29–34; Leslie Fiedler, "The New Mutants," *Partisan Review* 32 (Fall 1965): 505–25, and "Cross the Border—Close that Gap," in *American Literature Since 1900*, ed. Marcus Cunliffe (London: Barrie and Jenkins, 1975) 344–66; Jürgen Habermas, "Modernity—An Incomplete Project," in *The Anti-Aesthetic: Essays on Postmodern Culture*, ed. Hal Foster (Port Townsend: Bay Press, 1983); Ihab Hassan, "POSTmodernISM," *New Literary History* 3 (Autumn 1971): 5–30, and *The Dismemberment of Orpheus: Toward a Postmodern Literature* (New York: Oxford UP, 1971), and "The New Gnosticism: Speculations on an Aspect of the Postmodern Mind," *Boundary 2* 1 (Spring 1973): 547–69; Irving Howe, "Mass Society and Post-Modern Fiction," *Partisan Review* 26 (Summer 1959): 420–36; Frank Kermode, *Continuities* (London: Routledge and Kegan Paul, 1968); Richard Kostelanetz, *On Contemporary Literature* (New York: Avon, 1964); Harry Levin, "What Was Modernism?" *Massachusetts Review* 1 (Aug. 1960): 609–30, reprinted in *Refractions* (New York: Oxford UP, 1966); Jean-François Lyotard, *The Postmodern Condition: A Report on Knowledge*, trans. Geoff Bennington and Brian Massumi (Minneapolis: U of Minnesota P, 1984); Philip Rahv, *The Myth and the Powerhouse* (New York: Farrar, Straus, and Giroux, 1965); Susan Sontag, *Against Interpretation* (New York: Farrar, Straus, and Giroux, 1966); Stephen Spender, *The Struggle of the Modern* (London: Hamish Hamilton, 1963).

live in an age, Liu says, in which the study of history and of culture is committed to "particularism, localism, regionalism, relative autonomism, incommensurabilism, accidentalism (or contingency), anecdotalism . . . and 'micro-,' 'hetero-,' and 'poly'-ism,"[38] and the description of realities conceived on these premises can only be given in such characteristic postmodern forms as the matrix, the array, or the list—forms, that is, that present an aggregate of particulars without ordering them.

It is not simply that the multiplicity and diversity of particulars precludes intellectual grasp of them, but also that the literary historian deliberately resists grasping them totally. Moreover, in the view of postmodernist cultural criticism, each particular is itself inhabited by indeterminacy, for each must be interpreted and, hence, can be seen from multiple perspectives and bear innumerable different meanings. Thus the heterogeneity of a postmodern period reflects the premises its interpreters would also apply to any other age.

The age cannot be grasped in generalizations both because it is (said to be) incoherent and because the would-be generalizers are committed to incoherence as a method of presentation. Since we have no way of knowing, however, whether our age is "really" more incoherent than past ages or not, we must ask why we prefer to insist that it is. If we assume that our age is, in fact, less diverse and more homogenized than previous ones, we would suggest an answer. The localism, incommensurabilism, and so forth, on which academic cultural commentators insist, would be an ideological veil to the worldwide rationalization, modernization, and increasing sameness of forms of life.

If we applied Hayden White's scheme that derives every historical narrative from one of four tropes,[39] irony

---

[38] Alan Liu, "Local Transcendence: Cultural Criticism, Postmodernism, and the Romanticism of Detail," *Representations* 32 (Fall 1990): 78.

[39] Hayden White, *Metahistory: The Historical Imagination in*

is the one that pervades my narrative of the construction of English romantic poetry as a classification. Wellek, in contrast, plots the story as the gradual discovery of truths about English poetry in the early nineteenth century—its true leading characteristics and its true essential unity. My narrative exhibits a kaleidoscope or, more precisely, a carousel of changing critical views, and it nowhere suggests that one view is more correct than another or that time brings a better insight. Neither does it commit itself to the critical comedy that welcomes diversity as pluralism.

Moreover, while it tries to explain why we classify the poets together and call them romantic, the narrative also undermines confidence in this classification by showing that it was produced by contingencies. I could speculate as to what desires may be satisfied by this skepticism. But even though we live in an age of confession, such surmises are better left to others. I merely remark that our struggles are mostly with ourselves, and a person probably does not take an ironical view of intellectual history unless he wants to take a more positive one.

How, then, shall we decide the historical questions at issue? Are important features of the poetry of Wordsworth, Shelley, Byron, and the other poets to be explained by their reactions to the French Revolution? And if so, were these reactions essentially similar, so that they provide a ground for classifying the poets together and considering them as a group? To both of the latter questions, several contemporaries of the poets, such as Francis Jeffrey, William Hazlitt, and John Wilson, answered affirmatively. So also did several Victorian critics. Their position was revived in our time by M. H. Abrams and is now widely accepted as a premise.

Or should we adopt, instead, the view of Dowden and Hancock at the end of the nineteenth century? They held

Nineteenth-Century Europe (Baltimore: Johns Hopkins UP, pbk., 1975) 31–42.

that all the poets were deeply influenced by the French
Revolution but that its impact on them and on their
poetry was widely different in each case. Hence, if we
speak of them as a group, the French Revolution cannot
be the ground of this synthesis. Jerome McGann, Alan
Liu, and many other scholars hold this view at present.
They see poems as responses to political or social reality
but emphasize the extent to which these responses are
particularized and differentiated.

Or should we believe, with Watts-Dunton, Beers, Herford, Vaughan, and most authorities in the field from the
1890s through the 1950s, that the diverse literature that
we now call romantic poetry is not to be explained by the
French Revolution and that, instead, its causes are to be
found in intellectual and cultural trends that became
prominent in the eighteenth century? To my mind such
questions are unanswerable. More exactly, they cannot be
finally resolved by objective methods of historiography,
and the positions taken will reflect general ideological
convictions. If one sees the alternative narratives that are
possible, and the reasons why at various times one or
another has been preferred, no narrative can be simply or
wholly believable.

Yet after they have constructed their narratives, most
literary historians believe them. Their sense of conviction rests, I believe, on grounds that may broadly be
called aesthetic. They have integrated many events into a
pattern, and the sense of totality and coherence trans-
forms itself into a sense of truth.

From what has been said in this chapter and the last,
it seems that literary classifications have little plausibility. They do not represent past realities, and only the
naive could believe that they do. For how can groupings
of books and authors that are based on the inertia of tradition, on the mere say-so of authors vying with each
other for notice, on the uncertain perceptions of literary
historians, on their need to construct formal symmetries,

and on external facts—in other words, not on the objects to be classified but on circumstances adjacent to them— have credibility? Or how can a classification formed by contingency after contingency, as was shown in the case of English romantic poetry, have authority for us? Even Dilthey became anxious when he tried to ground and delimit logical subjects. "The problem is, what form it [history] takes when . . . statements are to be made about subjects that are in some sense interconnections of persons . . . where a boundary is not given in the unity of a personal life, [how is it possible] to find firm demarcations in this boundless interplay of individual existence. It is as though lines should be drawn in a constantly flowing river."[40]

Of course, there are differences between the literary texts of, say, 1790 and those of 1990. Reading the texts for the first time, one could place them in their periods. But the objects to be classified are heterogeneous; in observing their similarities and differences we must be selective; in drawing the boundary lines we must impose a single point of view or a limited set of points of view. In the process of being formed, classifications cease adequately to represent the past. In this failure, the other determinants of classifications I described, the ones additional to the desire for objective accuracy, have room to riot, and classifications become ideological, aesthetic, merely traditional, and motivated by career interests or by whim.

Despite the grip of tradition, classifications may change enormously over time. Thanks to the contemporary women's movement, Mary Sidney, Lady Mary Worth, Amelia Lanyer, and Elizabeth Cary are now not only recognized writers but belong to an accepted classification— Renaissance women writers. Even though the cockney

---

[40] Wilhelm Dilthey, *Der Aufbau der geschichtlichen Welt in den Geisteswissenschaften, Gesammelte Schriften* (Leipzig: Teubner, 1936) 7:280.

label pointed to elements in Keats that must be recognized and assimilated, most of us would be shocked if Keats were now classified with the Cockney school of poets (i.e., with such contemporaries of his as Leigh Hunt and John Hamilton Reynolds). For the classification embodies the snobbish values of a social world that is gone. The ideology that produced it conflicts with our own. Even if this were not the case, the classification could not be used. The enormously favorable reception of Keats since the Pre-Raphaelites necessitates a more honorific classification based on other qualities of his verse. For similar reasons, most of us would not now cite the class position of the characters in a drama as a feature by which we discriminate genres, such as tragedy from comedy. Classifications reflect the times that produce them and change as the times change.

Should we not, then, simply agree with Croce that literary classifications are at best practical conveniences, tools of exposition, helpful for certain jobs, such as surveys of a field? Depending on which features of a text we emphasize, we place it in different classifications. "Every genuine work of art," Croce typically remarks, "is at the same time naturalistic and symbolic, idealistic, Classical and Romantic."[41] Our classifications vary with our interests, with the questions we ask about texts, with the aims we pursue. Any classification is valid if it is anchored in some features of the texts.

Yet to me this deconstruction seems, in our present historical moment, too easy and predictable to be quite acceptable. We must ask whether there are criteria that would allow us to make distinctions, to judge that one classification has more validity than another. The rules of the discipline—that judgments must be backed up by arguments, that they must be consistent with each other, that sources must be criticized, that relevant facts cannot

---

[41] Quoted in Gian N. G. Orsini, *Benedetto Croce: Philosopher of Art and Literary Critic* (Carbondale: Southern Illinois UP, 1961) 51.

be ignored—provide one set of criteria. For some persons these criteria are invalid because they are ideological in the sense of a false consciousness. Certainly they presuppose an ontology and epistemology that need not be credited and is not universal. However, I addressed this issue in the first chapter and shall think now within the ideology (if it is that) of the discipline.

Tradition in literary classification need not be merely blind inertia. It can be modeled positively, as a self-corrective dialogue that continues over generations. Once a classification exists, its concept and canon are continually tested against each other in a process that gradually modifies both. As a literary historian groups texts, he compares them with each other and with a taxonomic concept. He is reasoning in a hermeneutic circle. In its negative aspect, reasoning in a hermeneutic circle means that we cannot know what texts are to be classified as romantic, for example, unless we have a concept of romanticism. Yet we must derive the concept from romantic texts. But in fact we come into the hermeneutic circle at a certain point, that is, we always find ourselves furnished with preconceptions. A role of cultural tradition in taxonomy is to supply such beginning points, and a role of external facts is also to do this and, additionally, to ground the taxonomy in historical realities.

The role of reasoning within a hermeneutic circle is to correct the preconceptions. The literary historian reads texts in the light of a taxonomic (pre)conception, and this evokes a nexus of expectations about the texts. If a text does not fully correspond to these expectations, he may conclude either that the text does not belong in this particular classification or that his conception of this category should be revised. In the latter case, he will reread the text in the light of his revised conception. If there is still a discrepancy, the conception must again be revised.

The process of adjusting the concept to the text is not completely open and unprejudiced, since preconceptions determine to some extent what one sees in the text and tend thus to be confirmed. But this is only a tendency, and as they try to apply a concept to a text, literary taxonomers typically encounter difficulties. The labor and anxiety these cause are all the greater because classification requires that the same concept fit many texts. The process I just described must be repeated over and over, with text after text, and it must finally result in a classification concept that, in theory, applies well and equally to all the texts that are included under the concept. Of course, this never happens in fact.

If we consider literary history as an institution, a collective process carried forward through generations, the process of taxonomizing can be viewed as, over time, dialectical and open-ended. Within the preselected set of texts, the taxonomic concept derived from one text is applied to another, modified to fit the second text, and then revised again to fit both texts. The same process is repeated with the third, fourth, and fifth texts, and so on indefinitely. It may happen that, as the concept is modified, it no longer fits one or more of the texts formerly included under the concept. These will be deleted from the taxonomic set.

It also happens that, as a concept is revised, it fits texts that would not have come under the original concept. Thus the concept changes because the set of texts does, and the set of texts changes because the concept does, and large modifications in both take place over time. Though this process can never completely transcend its beginning, it is self-correcting and, if there were no other factors involved, would tend toward stable categories and consensus.

Moreover, when the same set of texts is retaxonomized by successive literary historians, they may come to the same results even though they are working from different points of view. The fact does not necessarily illustrate the might of tradition but may, instead, indicate that the existing groupings have convincing grounds in the texts themselves. A taxonomy that has withstood the pressure of many reexaminations might be granted a certain authority. As Gadamer puts it, a tradition does not persist merely by cultural inertia; "preservation is also an act of reason, though one, to be sure, that is characterized by its inconspicuousness."[42]

But the strongest argument that a classification has validity must be drawn from its historical impact. In other words, when a classification has been active in forming works, it is grounded in realities of past life. For brevity, I develop this argument only with reference to the classification of authors into groups. But a closely similar argument could be deployed to justify reference to genres, traditions, and periods. A sorting by genre is valid if the concept of the genre was entertained by the writer and his contemporary readers. For in this case the expectations associated with the concept were effective in forming both the work and the responses to it. It is reasonable to place Pope in the tradition of Dryden, or Allen Ginsberg with Whitman, since the writers viewed themselves in this way, and this view shaped their styles. The concepts and boundaries of periods are valid if persons living at the time define it as a period, and if the period concept has real effects in determining the character of texts.

In the modern world, and even to some extent in earlier periods, writers tend to classify themselves. They state their influences and affinities, and very often they present themselves to readers as members of a group: the Pléiade, Sons of Ben, Parnassians, Pre-Raphaelites, aesthetes, Futurists, Imagists, Objectivists, Gruppe 47. Writers have many psychological and career motivations for doing this, and in the modern world these acts of self-classification also testify to the role and authority of literary history in our society. When a writer classifies himself, he places himself within literary history. Thus, implicitly, he prefers a claim for survival and attempts to

---

[42] Hans-Georg Gadamer, *Wahrheit und Methode* (Tübingen: J. C. B. Mohr, 1986) 286.

define the terms in which literary history will characterize him.

Yet along with all the other motives for forming
groups, it may happen that writers sense affinities with
each other. They feel they belong together. In this case,
the classification is simply a generalization of their feeling. That an author identifies with a group does not
mean, of course, that the identification is total or that it
lasts throughout his life. He shares the material circumstances, problems, predecessors, influences, interests,
ideals, aims, values, and whatever else that connects the
group, but each member does so variously and perhaps
only for a period of time. Nevertheless, up to some point,
the circumstances and aims of the group are his; when
we speak of the group, we are speaking, mutatis mutandis, of him also. If we start with the individual, we can
move to the group through the concept of participatory
belonging.

There may also be a reception and impact of the group
as such. This is especially likely when the group presents
itself in joint publications, such as anthologies. But what
most brings this about are programmatic statements by
the group and critical conceptualizations of it. Such writings speak of the group as an entity and attribute to it a
history, *Weltanschauung*, set of aims, and so forth. Thus,
they lead readers to perceive and react to a group (or to a
concept of one) rather than to an aggregate of different
writers. The many American poets who were intrigued
by Imagism, and wrote in that style, were not modeling
their work on particular poems so much as they were
adopting a program, communicated to them by anthologies, manifestoes, and critical advocacy.

In this and similar cases, the use of the classification
(Imagism) in a literary history is based on similarities
among texts, and the perception of these similarities by
the literary historian is activated by knowledge of external facts; that is, the historian knows that the Imagist
poets felt themselves to be a group and were so viewed by

their contemporaries. Similarities among texts resulted from the unified impact of the group on the genesis of texts, and this impact was due to the concept of the group. Thus the processes of creating a classification have effects on the literature that is produced, and these effects provide a basis for the classification.

This group reception and impact does not happen only with contemporaries. One thinks of T. S. Eliot's critical essays characterizing the Metaphysical poetry of the seventeenth century, or of Arthur Symons's *The Symbolist Movement in Literature*. That writers have at some time been classified as a group does not of course mean that we always continue to use this classification. Thus we no longer refer to Metaphysical poets, because Eliot's characterization of the style and mentality of this supposed group applies, as it currently seems to us, only to Donne. (Eliot was under the necessity of perceiving a school of poets because he wanted to make them typical of the seventeenth-century mind, which he wished to contrast with the modern mind.) But Eliot's classification of Metaphysical poets had effects on modern poetry. Hence, though we do not speak of a metaphysical school in the seventeenth century, we may still group poets of the "metaphysical revival" in the twentieth century. That Eliot's critical essays caused poets to imitate certain qualities of Donne produced similarities in their texts.

I cannot agree with Croce that literary classifications are in all cases merely practical conveniences or conventions or that we can group texts and authors in any way we like with equal legitimacy or lack of it. It is clear that classifications must address our present interests and must therefore change as the present does. Yet a classification that is merely perspectival, that reflects merely the points of view of readers in the present, would be self-contradictory in a literary history, since it attempts to describe the past. Between present and past perspectives, the mediating factor is of course tradition. Our present perspectives are formed not only by the needs and interests of the present but also by the past. Tradition is our term for the processes that carry the past into our present lives, shaping them.

To sum up: in the process of classifying groups, schools, movements, and so on, we may gather certain authors together because they themselves and their contemporaries felt that they belonged together. To classify them together is justified by the principle of participatory belonging. It is further justified if they had an effect on literary history as a group, as evidenced by the study of impact or reception. The group as such may be said to have had a real existence in the course of events, to have been a cause. Meanwhile, the reading of their works may reveal similarities of style, theme, and *Weltanschauung*, and these affinities between them may be greater than we see with other writers not in their group, while the differences are less. This, admittedly, must be a subjective judgment. Furthermore, it must be a prejudiced one, since we started with the assumption that they were a group.

Yet the judgment may be confirmed by successive generations of literary historians, viewing from very different contexts. When a classification fulfills these criteria of referring to a group that felt itself to be a group, was effective in history as a group, and created what seems to us a genuine synthesis of works, it is as valid as a literary classification can be. With these criteria we can measure the relative degree of justification for the various classifications that are used. It is, therefore, possible to classify wrongly or badly, and all classifications are not equally valid or arbitrary. By these criteria, English romantic poetry seems to me a classification that is not well grounded; Imagist poetry seems a relatively acceptable one.

Of course, the validity of a classification lies ultimately in similarities among the texts it gathers together. When all has been said that can be said in favor of tradition, it can only propose a classification weightily; it cannot confirm its correctness. So also with external facts. For example, authors may perceive resemblances among the texts they severally produce, but a literary historian may think their perceptions wrong. Since the question comes finally down to perceptions, any classification can be deconstructed. For obviously, texts are different, however similar they may also be. Whether a classification will be adopted and used or deconstructed depends on the literary historian's general premises, institutional interests, politics, and so forth. Nevertheless, if such factors are in the end decisive, this end is at some distance. Both as we think about literary classification in a metacritical way and as we practice it, the criteria I mention above are usually allowed their important role. They include quasi-objective reasons for or against the acceptance of a given classification.

6

The Explanation of Literary Change: Historical Contextualism

THUS FAR WE HAVE CONSIDERED WHAT MIGHT BE called the organizing of a literary history—the selecting, interrelating, structuring, interpreting, and presenting of information. First the works or authors must be grouped. There is no possibility of ordering the field or understanding what it contains until the multitude of discrete entities are reduced through classification to fewer ones. After grouping the works in the field, a literary historian must choose a major form in which to present results. I have argued that literary histories have two major forms, encyclopedic and narrative. I also have called attention to conceptual literary history as a subdivision of narrative. In this type, the historical field is integrated on the basis of a concept (or system of concepts) that the works are said to illustrate. Many such literary histories trace the fortunes of a concept, its changing character, or its reception over time.

We turn now from the problems of organizing history to those of explaining it. An explanation tells why and how texts acquire the characteristics they have, and why they vary from previous texts in the specific ways they do. Reason might suggest that a good literary style would continue forever. Since history belies reason, and styles change, we try to account for the fact.

Organizing literary history and explaining it are of course intimately related. A narrative reports, for example, that the novel became less popular because film was invented. *A* happened, causing *B*, which led to *C*. Some theorists hold that a narrative can be an adequate explanation of the events it includes. In encyclopedic literary histories, explanations are necessarily incomplete, dispersed, and ad hoc. In the past, encyclopedic form was a lazy convenience. But in contemporary literary histories, the form may be adopted precisely because the historian feels that no total explanation is possible.

At the present time, virtually all explanations in literary histories are contextual. In other words, the historian places the text or textual feature that is to be explained in a set of other texts or circumstances that are said to have caused it or that help account for it. The context may be used to explain not only features of the text, but also its qualitative merit. Already in antiquity, the worth of the literature of Athens in the fifth century was explained by the free, democratic institutions of that city. The difference between explanations depends partly on what area of context is foregrounded—literature as an institution, other discourses, sociological structures, the economic order, political history. And it also depends on the mode of relationship—organic, oppositional, and so on—that is assumed to exist between the context and the text.

The terms *context* and *text* are problematic. We experience the text as a nexus of meanings, and which ones are in the text and which derive from the context cannot be strictly determined. In any act of interpretation, the borders between the textual and the contextual are drawn by convention. Nevertheless, no one denies that texts are interpreted in contexts. Despite the difficulties, the terms refer to different moments in the processes of interpreting and accounting for literary works.

The examples of contextual literary history chosen for comment are, in chronological order, Robert Wood's *Essay on the Original Genius of Homer* (1769); Wilhelm Dilthey's 1865 essay on Novalis in *Das Erlebnis und die Dichtung*; Sandra Gilbert and Susan Gubar's *The Mad-*

woman in the Attic (1979); Stephen Greenblatt's *Shake-spearean Negotiations* (1988); and Alan Liu's *Words-worth: The Sense of History* (1989). That this group seems unrelated is of course intentional. The aim is to represent quite different varieties of contextual literary history, yet to show that the limitations and aporias inherent in the method are evident in all. Any set of examples would substantiate essentially the same points.

Robert Wood is cited as one of the first persons to apply in a systematic way what is still the most common and, intuitively, the most probable type of contextual explanation, namely, that a literary work directly reflects the world its author lives in. More than any other single thinker, Dilthey provides the intellectual foundations for literary history as it was generally written from the later nineteenth century until the end of the Second World War and, in particular, for *Geistesgeschichte.* His essays in *Das Erlebnis und die Dichtung* are his most important practical attempts in the genre. The final three books exemplify literary history in the United States in its present moment of crisis.

Feminist literary history has altered our picture of the past more than any other type of literary history in my lifetime, and I cite the work of Gilbert and Gubar as a well-known example. Its assumptions are essentially those of Wood—that a literary text expresses its author's mind and feelings and that these are formed and shaped by personal experiences. Gilbert and Gubar argue that the experience of living in a patriarchal society determines women's feelings in important ways and that these feelings are shared by all women writers. Among works by younger scholars, Liu's book offers an exceptionally probing and sophisticated attempt to relate the genesis of literary texts to social circumstances and political history. In his opinion, literature does not directly express or reflect these factors but does so in an ideologically deflected way. As well as any single book could, Greenblatt's illustrates the peculiarities of Renaissance New Historicism. Among our literary historians at present, moreover, Greenblatt offers an especially plausible, though vague, vision of the social processes by which literature is engendered—the contextual processes that explain texts.

Certain axioms are fundamental to contextualizing explanation as a method.[1] That context shapes texts is an assumption that empowers the method and cannot itself be proved. In a typical example, Jochen Schulte-Sasse discusses the hesitations of Weislingen, in Goethe's *Götz von Berlichingen,* between "the old, feudal independence and the court life. To explain his hesitation by his character will not in the least do justice to his semantic function. He is the symbol of historical change, a figure of transition."[2]

If we ask why psychological analysis cannot adequately account for Weislingen's hesitations, there is no answer except that historical contextualism prefers its own mode of explanation. It prompts research into the context and shows the possible relevance of the context in the particular case. It cannot demonstrate the irrelevance of alternative, noncontextual considerations to explain the same features of a text. Moreover, since contextual explanations pertain only to particular texts, no amount of them can justify a conclusion that context is *always* determining.

---

[1] For discussion of contextualizing explanation in the writing of history, see Hayden White, *Metahistory: The Historical Imagination in Nineteenth-Century Europe* (Baltimore: Johns Hopkins UP, pbk., 1975) 17–21; in intellectual history, see Dominick LaCapra, "Rethinking Intellectual History and Reading Texts," in *Modern European Intellectual History: Reappraisals and New Perspectives,* ed. Dominick LaCapra and Steven L. Kaplan (Ithaca: Cornell UP, 1982) 47–86, reprinted in Dominick LaCapra, *Rethinking Intellectual History: Texts, Contexts, Language* (Ithaca: Cornell UP, 1983) 23–71; and in intellectual life generally, see White's source in Stephen Pepper, *World Hypotheses: A Study in Evidence* (Berkeley: U of California P, 1942) 232–79.

[2] Jochen Schulte-Sasse, "Drama," in *Hansers Sozialgeschichte der deutschen Literatur vom 16. Jahrhundert bis zur Gegenwart,* vol. 3, *Deutsche Aufklärung bis zur Französischen Revolution 1680–1789,* ed. Rolf Grimminger (Munich: Carl Hanser, 1980) 479.

Another axiom is that the context of any text is unsearchably extensive and can never be fully described or known. The threads from the text into the context extend on all sides and lead, in Hayden White's metaphor, into "different areas of context" (18), stretching always further than they can be traced. In principle, contextual explanation cannot confine itself to only one or a few areas of context, though invariably this happens in practice. "There are," says Stephen Pepper, "many equally revealing ways of analyzing an event, depending simply on what strands you follow from the event into the context. At each stage of your analysis . . . this choice of what strand to follow comes up again, and every strand is more or less relevant" (250). We decide which strands to follow on some basis, obviously, but whatever basis it may be, it will not be the principle of contextual explanation, for this would lead us to follow all strands.[3]

This point was clear from the start of literary history, and is well stated by Dilthey: "Here, however, the true way in which we handle the historical conditions is to be emphasized. We leave the greater part of them entirely out of account, and without further consideration treat a limited set, that we select from them, as the totality. If, then, we claim to represent the historical conditions in our analysis, our claim, already on this ground, can only be approximately correct. We explain only by the most obvious conditions."[4]

A basic problem of contextual explanation is to maintain a ground for both the similarity and the difference between literary works. Sophisticated literary historians are keenly aware of the problem and have developed vari-

[3] Max Weber, "'Objectivity' in Social Science and Social Policy," *The Methodology of the Social Sciences*, trans. Edward A. Shils and Henry A. Finch (New York: Free Press, 1949) 78–84, discusses some of the general considerations that may lead us to foreground one aspect of context rather than another.

[4] Wilhelm Dilthey, *Das Erlebnis und die Dichtung*, 12th ed. (Göttingen: Vandenhoeck and Ruprecht, 1921) 171.

ous expedients, but essentially the problem is insoluble. There must be similarities between works to justify grouping them together (in genres, periods, traditions, movements, discursive practices, and so on), for without classification and generalization, the field cannot be grasped mentally. A great many, perfectly heterogeneous objects cannot be understood. Neither can they be represented within the amount of pages available to even the amplest of literary histories. On the other hand, we must obviously preserve the differences between works if only because these correspond to our sense of truth.

If we start with the context, we cannot explain how it could determine works to be different. This consideration makes difficulties for classic Marxist explanations and also, as we shall see, for the explanation of qualitative differences between texts.[5] In other words, if works have the same context, yet are unlike, their dissimilarities cannot be explained contextually. Some other explanatory principle must be allowed. This happens all the time in literary histories (usually the other principle is the genius, temperament, or innate psychology of the writer), but such methodological compromise or unrigorous eclecticism brings the discipline into intellectual dishonor. Purists also hold that a literary history should explain by only one area of context—by sociological factors, for example, or by *Geistesgeschichte*—and should not foreground now one area of context and now another.

On the other hand, if we start with the differences between texts, we must, as contextualizers, look for dis-

---

[5] H. R. Jauss, *Toward an Aesthetic of Reception*, trans. Timothy Bahti (Minneapolis: U of Minnesota P, 1982) 12, comments on this dilemma of classic Marxist explanations: "Since the number of ascertainable determinants in the 'infrastructure' remained incomparably smaller than the more rapidly changing literary production of the 'superstructure,' the concrete multiplicity of works and genres had to be traced back to always the same factors or conceptual hypotheses, such as feudalism, the rise of the bourgeois society, the cutting-back of the nobility's function, and early, high, or late capitalist modes of production."

similarities in their contexts that would explain these divergencies. Thus we construct a different context for each text. Of course, both texts and contexts can in fact be both similar and dissimilar at the same time, resembling each other in some respects and not in others. But in the writing of literary history, fashion swings over time from one pole to the other, and literary historians currently emphasize the diversity of contexts—locale, class, profession, institution, and so on—that were present in the tract of time they analyze.

Whatever the object of historical inquiry, it is analyzed into heterogeneous objects, conflicting instances. This procedure is often advocated and practiced in a self-righteous, self-congratulatory mood, as though it were an anti-ideological, antiestablishment gesture. We should keep in mind that what this historiography dissolves is not merely traditional and suspect images of the past (E. M. W. Tillyard's description of *The Elizabethan World Picture* has often been cited as an example) but the possibility of forming any picture of the past at all, of holding it in mind, of understanding it.

I should like to comment on certain consequences of these dilemmas. A literary history loses focus on texts if it tries to exhibit much of their context. This causes acute practical difficulties in the writing of literary histories. On the one hand, literature must not be engulfed and lost from view in representations of the total historical process of which literature is a part.[6] On the other hand, the social and historical context must not be relegated to an introduction or to separate chapters or parts of the book. For, in this case, the context inevitably becomes background, that is, a nexus of data loosely related to the texts themselves, the reader being required to do most of the relating.

[6] Rolf Grimminger, "Vorbemerkung," in *Hansers Sozialgeschichte* 8–9; René Wellek and Austin Warren, *Theory of Literature* (New York: Harcourt, Brace, 1942) 264.

It is, in fact, difficult for a literary history to represent the contextual realities as a sophisticated literary historian conceives them. How can an essay or book adequately display the intricate, manifold involvement of a particular text in the hugely diverse context that is thought to determine it? Moreover, any context we use for interpretation or explanation must itself be interpreted.[7] In other words, the context must be put in a wider context, which itself must be interpreted contextually, and so on in a recession that can only be halted arbitrarily.[8]

For practical reasons, therefore, each book or article describes only a small piece of the context. But then a convincing argument must be given for privileging the bit of context we choose, a step often omitted. The procedure is necessarily reductive.[9] As we juxtapose our selected bit of context with the text, the wide spectrum of possible explanations dwindles to whatever our piece of context can support. Yet we try to make the piece of context support as much as possible and so fall into strained ingenuity and implausibility. The same logic imposes itself, of course, when we make contextual interpretations of texts. Historical contextualism tends to suppress critical intelligence.

Qualitative differences between texts raise these issues with special force. That historical contextualism,

---

[7] Compare Jane P. Tomkins, "Graff Against Himself," *Modern Language Notes* 96 (Dec. 1981): 1095: "If it is true that historical description . . . or any set of agreed upon historical facts are themselves the product of interpretation, how can we call upon history . . . to provide a ground against which the figure of the text may stand in relief?"

[8] Compare Uwe Japp, *Beziehungssinn: Ein Konzept der Literaturgeschichte* (Frankfurt a. M.: Europäische Verlagsanstalt, 1980) 68: "If every signification can be understood only under the condition that one understands it within its contextual frame, this would in turn require that one draw in the next higher contextual frame. This would be no infinite regression, but a finite one, because every explication of a significance must finally reach the widest possible context."

[9] Jean E. Howard, "The New Historicism in Renaissance Studies," *English Literary Renaissance* 16 (Winter 1986): 24, 31, 41.

the reference to political, economic, sociological, cultural, and literary circumstances, has no power to explain or even to describe the greater value of *Othello* than of Dekker's *The Honest Whore* or of Keats's volume of 1820 than of John Hamilton Reynolds's of 1821 is, to say the least, a serious deficiency. Historical contextualism may suggest conditions that enabled the achievement of Shakespeare or Keats and determined the forms and contents of their works, but it cannot explain the achievement itself, the worth. Unless it asserts that they were produced in different contexts, it can find no cause why one work is better than another. Yet the quality or value of a work is usually the reason for seeking to contextualize it. As they emphasize some authors or texts rather than others, literary historians depend on qualitative judgments, but their methods provide no criteria for making such judgments.

To discuss how canons are made would be a digression, but I may at least notice the opinion that they are always primarily ideological. For if this were the whole or even the main story, historical contextualism might indeed explain why Shakespeare and Keats occupy more space in literary histories than Dekker or Reynolds. The historian would show that in the ideological struggles of the years when Keats became canonical, his poems served politically dominant interests or, so far as was possible, were interpretively appropriated to do so. This argument gets the cart before the horse. Authors who have become canonical are ideologically appropriated, and this appropriation is one reason why they continue to be canonical. "Even the dead," as Benjamin says, "are not safe from the enemy when he conquers."[10] But they are appropriated because they are becoming canonical, and in the rise to canonicity, ideology is not decisive. It may hinder accep-

[10] Walter Benjamin, "Über den Begriff der Geschichte," *Gesammelte Schriften*, ed. R. Tiedemann and H. Schweppenhäuser (Frankfurt a. M.: Suhrkamp, 1974) 1:695.

tance, as with Ezra Pound, but does not of itself cause it.

The poems of Reynolds and Keats do not differ in their ideological availability. If Keats is appropriated and Reynolds forgotten, the difference must lie in qualities of Keats's poetry other than its ideological appeal. These, then, are the decisive factors in the processes by which his reputation was formed. To assert that our enthusiasms and ennuis in reading are determined mainly by ideology is belied by the common experience of being moved and delighted by texts that are ideologically poisonous to us.

The most detailed study of canon formation known to me is Peter Uwe Hohendahl's *Building a National Literature: The Case of Germany, 1830–1870.*[11] As Hohendahl closely analyzes the impact of political commitments and ideologies on critical opinions and the building of the canon, he bears out my argument. For example, Goethe was ideologically appropriated by different groups, but he was already canonical in the first important history of German literature by Gervinus (1835–42). Hohendahl explains the ideological functions Gervinus made Goethe serve. He does not, and does not have to, explain why Gervinus cast Goethe, rather than some other writer, in the important role.

We cannot describe a context and from it predict the characteristics of the texts it will determine.[12] We start with the text and then construct a context to explain it. Whatever context a literary historian presents, the same textual characteristics can always be accounted for by alternative contextual explanations. For example, the formal discontinuity and fragmentation in *The Waste Land* can be related to Eliot's reading of F. H. Bradley and

---

[11] Peter Uwe Hohendahl, *Building a National Literature: The Case of Germany, 1830–1870,* trans. R. B. Franciscono (Ithaca: Cornell UP, 1989).

[12] R. S. Crane, *Critical and Historical Principles of Literary History* (Chicago: U of Chicago P, 1971) 22, points out that at most the circumstances of the age only create the possibility of producing the texts.

Freud, to film technique, to the impact of modern urban life on consciousness, to Eliot's class position, and so on. If the different contexts cannot be synthesized, as usually they can, we may not know which to prefer. Moreover, historical context almost invariably means, in practice, the world that was contemporary with the text when it was produced. Since writers also derive impulses from works of former ages, this contextualizing practice is simpleminded.[13] This difficulty can easily be avoided, but usually it is ignored, and intertextuality and history become rival ways of explaining texts.

Contextual explanation depends on a certain model of historical process. Between the context and the event it explains, a continuity or causal connection must be posited. Yet postmodern literary histories are generally committed to models of the real that posit discontinuity between events. They use contextual studies to dissolve historical generalizations. As they expose the weltering diversities and oppositions in the field of objects they consider, the continuities of traditional literary history vanish like ghosts at dawn. Thus context is deployed not to explain literary history but to deconstruct the possibility of explaining it. Yet the same historians also maintain that context is always only a construction of the literary historian, including, presumably, the context by which they deconstruct the context.

Two unresolved problems are mediation, to use the Marxist term, and the mode of relation between context and text. Theories of mediation try to answer the ques-

---

[13] René Wellek, "The Fall of Literary History," *The Attack on Literature and Other Essays* (Chapel Hill: U of North Carolina P, 1982) 75–76. Alastair Fowler makes this fact a point of disciplinary difference between history and literary history. See his "The Two Histories," in *Theoretical Issues in Literary History,* ed. David Perkins (Cambridge: Harvard UP, 1991) 123: "Very remote events . . . have usually no present effects worth discussing. . . . We can be fairly sure that a famine in ancient Sumeria has no immediate bearing on modern life." In literature, however, "literary classics may have direct effects after many centuries."

tion: how—by what paths, processes, or chain of events—does the context have its impact on the text?[14] Logically, this question is unanswerable, since between each link in the mediating chain mediations must be specified. The paths can never be completely traced. In too many literary histories, moreover, the attempt to trace mediations is scarcely made. Instead, a literary fact is merely juxtaposed with a fact of the social or political world, and the latter is asserted to be the cause of the former. The error here lies, as R. S. Crane puts it, in "the illicit assumption that we can deduce particularized actuality from general possibility" (53).

The problem of mediation becomes increasingly impossible as either the context or the event to be explained becomes larger and more amorphous. To say, as Lukács does, that the French Revolution and its attendant upheavals led to the creation of the historical novel as a form cannot be more than speculation.[15] Since mediation can never be proved, literary historians content themselves with probabilities. Whatever else is involved, in hypothesizing the paths of mediation we almost always give prominence to the mind of the author, conscious or or unconscious. Here the contextual phenomena are registered and transferred, so to speak, to the work of art.[16]

---

[14] Compare Colin Martindale, *Romantic Progressions: The Psychology of Literary History* (Washington, D. C.: Hemisphere, 1975) 9: "Although larger social changes may condition literary history, one cannot claim to have explained their effects until he has specified the *mechanisms* whereby the effect is generated."

[15] Georg Lukács, *The Historical Novel*, trans. Hannah and Stanley Mitchell (Lincoln: U of Nebraska P, 1983) 23–26.

[16] As Jan Mukařovský points out: "Personality is the point where all the external influences that can affect literature intersect; it is at the same time the focal point from which they enter literary development. Everything that takes place in literature happens by the mediation of personality." From "The Individual and the Development of Art," as quoted in Jurij Striedter, *Literary Structure, Evolution, and Value: Russian Formalism and Czech Structuralism Reconsidered* (Cambridge: Harvard UP, 1989) 117.

To ascribe such importance to the mind of the author is itself problematic; at the least, it is contrary to some theories of creativity. But the point I want to bring out is that, of itself, it makes mediation untraceable. We can observe what comes out of the minds of authors but not all that goes into them or goes on within them.

How to conceive the posture of the text vis-à-vis its context is hotly debated. Whether the text directly reflects or expresses its context, symbolically expresses it, negates it, deflects it, or has some other relation to it, the context may still be said to determine the text, but in other respects these theories may be very different. Of course, one might suggest that texts have various relations with contexts, and most literary histories are eclectic with respect to the kinds of context and the modes of relationship they deploy as explanations. But most theorists of literary history have posited a particular mode of relationship as the normal one. A typology of contextual explanations might be based on the area of context and the mode of relationship they privilege.

The areas of context usually cited are literary, cultural (*Geist*), or material, the latter being subdividable into the political, economic, and sociological. The modes in which texts can be related to these contexts are as simple mirrors or expressions, as symbolic, as organic parts of wholes, or as systematically differentiated. The latter category comprises theories that show how texts vary from their contexts in ways that the context determines.

Simple reflection or expression is, of course, the age-old assumption of mankind: texts express what the writers observed or felt in their historical world. This theory is by no means obsolete. It is assumed, for example, by Jochen Schulte-Sasse in his commentary on *Götz von Berlichingen* and by Sandra Gilbert and Susan Gubar in their analyses of the writings of women authors in the nineteenth century.

The most prominent theorist of organic relations between text and context is Hegel, but his assumptions, in modified form, were widely shared. Dilthey, for example, did not accept the teleological and mystical ideas of Hegel but held that, because of complex, specific circumstances, an idea may have a historical moment of prevalence. The ideal of reason, for example, was promulgated from mind to mind in the Enlightenment. It modified literary texts, legal procedures, political theory, and so on, because these interacted on each other, none having priority.[17] This type of *Geistesgeschichte*, which posits the unity of an age in the dominance of an idea, also describes an organic or part/whole relation of a text to its context.

Theories that emphasize the systematic difference of a text from its context include chiefly the various ones that conceive literature as an ideological reflection. We could also cite Fredric Jameson's theory, in *The Political Unconscious*, that art and literature express a formal and symbolic resolution of political and social contradictions.[18] In some theories, the relation of the text to its context is oppositional but not systematically so; that is, the respects in which the text diverges from its context are not determined by the context. In the complex dialectic of Adorno, for example, texts reflect social realities even—or especially—in their forms and structures. But as art, they also criticize and oppose society, preserving the utopian moment of reconciliation, though only as art's illusion.

In 1769, Robert Wood published his *Essay on the Original Genius of Homer*. Wood had traveled in Asia Minor and observed with interest that the "manners" and mentality he found there resembled the "representations of life" in the *Iliad*. He explains this by the continuity of physical and political structures that shaped existence in that part

---

[17] Wilhelm Dilthey, *Der Aufbau der geschichtlichen Welt in den Geisteswissenschaften* (Frankfurt a. M.: Suhrkamp, 1970) 188–89, 218–19.

[18] Fredric Jameson, *The Political Unconscious: Narrative as a Socially Symbolic Act* (Ithaca: Cornell UP, 1981) 79.

of the world—soil, climate, and despotism. Because of this continuity, he argues, we can use life there at present to interpret the *Iliad*. For example, "let us not" suppose, with some of Homer's "best Commentators, that he considered the passion of love as a weakness unworthy of a Hero. . . . This passion, according to our ideas of it, was unknown in the manners of that age . . . the female sphere of action . . . was then confined to the uniformity of servile domestic duties . . . [and] ideas of love extended little further than animal enjoyment."[19]

The resemblances between manners as we see them in the *Iliad* and as we see them now proved that Homer's "constant original manner of composition" (20) was to depict the world immediately about him. This bolstered some other deductions. Because the *Iliad* so accurately rendered the landscape about Troy, Wood felt that Homer must have lived "in the neighborhood of Troy" (197). "His manner, not only of describing actions and characters, but of drawing portraits, looks very much, as if he had been either present [at the siege of Troy], or at least had taken his information from eye-witnesses" (219).

By present lights, Wood's conclusions are entirely wrong. The manners described in the *Iliad* do not reflect any age exactly but a composite from different centuries. When what eventually became the *Iliad* was first written down, the poet or poets who dictated it were rendering a world they knew only from poems. Wood's brilliant essay can be cited as a permanent warning to historical contextualizers. It reminds us not to forget the role of tradition, convention, and stylization in literary creation. When Jerome McGann tells us that "everything about" Tennyson's "The Charge of the Light Brigade" is "time-and place-specific," and that, therefore, we should read the poem in the context of contemporary newspaper reports of the charge at Balaklava, I do not deny this, but I add that we

[19] Robert Wood, *An Essay on the Original Genius of Homer (1769 and 1775)* (Hildesheim: Georg Olms, 1976) 169.

should also read it within the traditions and conventions of heroic war poems, going as far back as the *Iliad*.[20]

Sandra Gilbert and Susan Gubar's *The Madwoman in the Attic* equally assumes that texts express what their authors experienced, and I comment on this assumption later. But the work also illustrates another point of much importance. When used to interpret literature, context is itself an interpretation. The works focused on are by women in the nineteenth century. The context is, on the one hand, the social and cultural situation of women then—the opportunities that were open or closed to them, the ideals of behavior prescribed for them, and so on. But as is typical and necessary in literary histories, the book merely alludes to these social and cultural factors in passing. No serious attempt is made to investigate them. The authors may have assumed that the facts are well known; they did not wish, in any case, to submerge their literary commentary in sociological data and argument. On the other hand, the context is the literature women read, which was predominantly by males but included a tradition of writings by women. This context consists, in the main, of Milton, of romantic poetry and gothic fiction, and of women writers. Additionally, Gilbert and Gubar exhibit images of women and attitudes to women writers that were, as they argue, generally present in literary tradition. In other words, the context is constructed very selectively. There is little reference to Shakespeare and to male novelists and essayists who were also contextually important.

The major effort of the book, so far as it is not mere commentary, is to infer the psychic reactions of women writers from the social and literary context. We must ask, then, how Gilbert and Gubar can ascertain what took place in the minds of women; what thoughts, emotions, processes, and defense mechanisms were activated with-

---

[20] Jerome McGann, *The Beauty of Inflections* (Oxford: Clarendon, 1985) 202.

in them? Gilbert and Gubar rely on what seems logically probable to them and in doing so, they project their own feelings onto past writers. They claim, for example, that Christina Rossetti and Emily Dickinson yearned for a lost mother country or sunken Atlantis of female community, a land where women authors were at home.[21]

On the evidence cited, this claim is unconvincing. What strikes one, in this literary history, is that history seems to have entailed so little change. Gilbert and Gubar assume that the social and psychic dilemmas of women writers did not alter essentially throughout the nineteenth century and have not since. Hence, they freely quote contemporaries, such as Anne Sexton and Adrienne Rich, to illuminate the states of mind of nineteenth-century women writers. In this respect, *The Madwoman in the Attic* is typical of feminist literary history and also of histories of literature by blacks, gays, and other minorities. Such histories promote feelings of identity and solidarity within the group by emphasizing continuities with the situation of members of the group in the past.

As they explore the psychological binds of women writers in a patriarchal society, Gilbert and Gubar also take guidance from the theories of Harold Bloom. The agonistic relations Bloom describes between writers become, in *The Madwoman in the Attic*, the desperation and swerves of women writers confronting male ones — their psychic strategies for coping with the anxiety of influence.

The assumption that literature articulates, directly or obliquely, the personal feelings and circumstances of the writer is not, to say the least, self-evident. As it is applied by Gilbert and Gubar, it seriously underestimates, in my opinion, the functioning of models, conventions, generic

[21] Sandra M. Gilbert and Susan Gubar, *The Madwoman in the Attic: The Woman Writer and the Nineteenth-Century Literary Imagination* (New Haven: Yale UP, 1979) 99–101.

repertoires, intertextuality, codes, the necessity of defamiliarization, and other formal considerations that determine literary works. Here I am only repeating the criticism I made of Wood and McGann. But the point I want to bring out is that the assumption is necessary to much feminist literary history. In fact, it is one of those assumptions that enables a discipline. If the interest of the literary historian is in the distinctive situation, emotions, and imagination of women, as evidenced by women writers, the texts must express what the historian seeks to know. Otherwise, why study them?

The Madwoman in the Attic reveals something that is generally true, mutatis mutandis, of all contextual literary histories. The contextualizing is, in a sense, bogus. The ideas by which the literary works are explained and interpreted are not derived from the contexts or the texts so much as they are imposed upon them. They are formed from other sources, in other experiences (for example, the experience of reading Harold Bloom), and applied to construct the contexts and read the texts. The ideas that Gilbert and Gubar apply in performing these constructions concern the psychic responses of women writers to social circumstances. This set of assumptions constitutes the critical machine that is created prior to reading the texts and is then driven over the texts and the contexts too.

A certain insensitivity or ruthlessness in the commentaries of Gilbert and Gubar makes this point especially visible. For example, both formal and ideological considerations lead Gilbert and Gubar to find madwomen among the characters in narratives by women. The formal necessity is visible in the title, which makes the madwoman a leitmotif of the book. Ideologically, there must be madwomen because this figure is "the *author's* double, an image of her own anxiety and rage" in a patriarchal society (78). It is assumed that all nineteenth-century women writers harbored these emotions. Consequently, a madwoman must be produced in the last chapter, on Emily Dickinson, and that she did not write narratives is no obstacle. Dickinson lived her life as "a kind of novel or narrative poem in which . . . [she] enacted and eventually resolved both her anxieties about her art and her anger at female subordination." In short, "Emily Dickinson herself became a madwoman" (583). This interpretation is not suggested by Dickinson's texts or by threads into their context, and yet *The Madwoman in the Attic* certainly intends to be contextual literary history.

Wilhelm Dilthey's 1865 essay on Novalis premises that writers come into the world with individual endowments—a temperament, psychological character, set of gifts—but if writers were only different from each other and not also like each other, it would be impossible to write a literary history. Members of the same generation encounter similar external conditions, Dilthey argues, and since these conditions partly determine their writings, resemblances arise, grounding the generalizations of literary history.[22]

External conditions, the world in which Novalis grew up, are, then, the context of his writings. They do not determine his writings completely, but negatively they close the horizon of what was possible for him. "The conditions contain within definite limits the variability of that which is formed."[23] In a very significant step, Dilthey divides "the conditions that affect the intellectual

---

[22] Rudolf Unger, *Literaturgeschichte als Problemgeschichte* (Berlin: Deutsche Verlagsgesellschaft für Politik und Geschichte, 1924) 7, says that Dilthey brought the idea of generations into *Geistesgeschichte*, taking the idea from his teacher, Ranke.

[23] Dilthey 171. Compare Fredric Jameson 148: "In the generic model outlined here, the relationship of the . . . historical situation to the text is not construed as causal . . . but rather as one of a limiting situation; the historical moment is here understood to block off or shut down a certain number of formal possibilities available before, and to open up determinate new ones. . . . Thus the *combinatoire* aims not at enumerating the 'causes' of a given text or form, but rather at mapping out its objective, a priori conditions of possibility, which is quite a different matter."

culture of a generation . . . into two factors." On the one hand, there is the "wealth of intellectual culture, as it is present at the time." On the other hand, there are the conditions of "surrounding life," the "social, political, and other circumstances of infinitely many kinds" (171). The latter limit the developments possible out of the former.

Thus, among the determinants of literary works, Dilthey gives special importance to cultural discourses. He does not provide an argument to show that culture or *Geist* is a primary component of the context. He just assumes it and embodies his assumption in the classification of contextual factors that presents *Geist* as half of the whole. In connection with Novalis, he stresses the philosophies of Kant, Jacobi, and Fichte, the writings of Goethe and Schiller, the ferment in the natural sciences, and the ideas and books of Novalis's contemporaries and friends — Schleiermacher, Friedrich and August Wilhelm Schlegel, and Ludwig Tieck. His essay, which is partly biographical, tells exactly how and when Novalis came into contact with these influences; and he is sometimes very particular, as when he devotes six pages to the impact of Goethe's *Wilhelm Meister* on Novalis's *Heinrich von Ofterdingen.*

On the subject of the material, social, and political conditions, however, Dilthey offers only a brief speculation. Germany, he argues, lacked a capital city, and in its small, moderately prosperous towns, the discoveries of the natural sciences had little effect on industry and trade. For similar reasons, the revolution in philosophy caused no changes in political, religious, or educational institutions. These conditions were deleterious for Novalis and other intellectuals of his generation. Since their ideas found no practical resonance, they did not sufficiently refer them to reality. With all their intellectual and formal brilliance, their works consequently suffered from overidealization, incompleteness, and unrootedness. They are a "shattering example" of the way "historical conditions keep nobly significant powers encircled as if with iron arms" (184).

The concept of a generation has often been used by literary historians, but the logic of it is demolished by Wellek, and it also invites postmodern deconstruction.[24] The most serious objection to Dilthey is, of course, that he overestimates the importance of *Geist* as a factor in the explanation of literary history. His position is opposite to that of Marx, and the one can be used to undermine the other. What for Dilthey is primary is for Marx secondary or superstructural; the material realities that for Marx are primary are for Dilthey a set of limiting conditions among other, equally limiting sets of conditions. All of these conditions restrict what can be in consciousness at a given time and thus they ground the possibility of literary history, but as negations, they still leave much open. If we were to ask Dilthey what determines works positively to become what they are, he would point to the potentialities for further development that are given in the existing stock of culture, but he would also note the innate gifts and differences of writers. In other words, he does not believe that texts are wholly determined by contexts, and he does not believe that the literary series can be completely explained.

By the middle of our century, most of the large, standard literary histories in England and the United States were more or less of Dilthey's kind. I do not mean that their authors had read Dilthey, for usually they had not. But they practiced a kind of historiography for which Dilthey is the most important theorist. The Anglo-Saxon literary historians of the 1940s and 1950s did not resemble Dilthey in giving central importance to biography, and they did not assert that periods are intellectually or spirit-

---

[24] See, for example, Friedrich Kummer, *Deutsche Literaturgeschichte des 19. Jahrhunderts dargestellt nach Generationen* (Dresden: C. Reissner, 1908); Julius Petersen, "Die literarischen Generationen," in *Philosophie der Literaturwissenschaft,* ed. Emil Ermatinger (Berlin: Junker and Dünnhaupt, 1930); Edward Wechssler, *Die Generation als Jugendreihe und ihr Kampf um die Denkform* (Leipzig: Quelle and Meyer, 1930). For Wellek's demolition see *Theory of Literature* 279–80.

ually unified. But like Dilthey they took the mind or thought of an age, as expressed in its philosophy, religion, science, law, educational theory, art, and literature, as their main explanatory context, and in contrast to many literary histories written in the Victorian period and in the present,[25] they granted the realm of mind or thought a large measure of autonomy. They doubted that changes in literature could usually be correlated with social, economic, and political developments and rarely attempted to make such connections. Much less did these literary historians suppose that literary and other discourses serve ideological functions in a struggle for social power. Two of the finer literary histories of the period can be cited as examples: the volumes in the *Oxford History of English Literature* by Douglas Bush, *English Literature in the Earlier Seventeenth Century 1600–1660* (1945), and C. S. Lewis, *English Literature in the Sixteenth Century Excluding Drama* (1954). They are quite different from works analyzed elsewhere in this chapter by present-day literary historians—Sandra Gilbert and Susan Gubar, Alan Liu, and Stephen Greenblatt.

Dilthey secured the unity of a period, which he grounded in a characteristic mentality, by emphasizing the newer developments in the intellectual life of a time and place. Only these were visible in his portraits of periods. Bush and Lewis, however, had a vision, which they did not articulate theoretically, that was more comparable to the structuralist vision of Braudel. For them the past lingered massively. Most of what was present in the sixteenth or seventeenth centuries was the past, that which had also been present in the Middle Ages.

In Bush and Lewis, this vision of historical reality was, in part, the natural product of a survey approach. If

[25] For a brief survey of Victorian literary histories, see René Wellek, "English Literary Historiography during the Nineteenth Century," in *Discriminations: Further Concepts of Criticism* (New Haven: Yale UP, 1970) 143–63.

we inventory what is thought at any given time, we will always find that most of it was also thought in earlier times. Also, both Bush and Lewis were reacting against previous descriptions of the Renaissance that too sharply demarcated and described it as an emancipation from the medieval. Their understanding of the slowness of general intellectual change and of the consequent diversity and strife of outlooks within their periods seemed in their time more sophisticated, learned, and balanced than the view it contested. What, in general, typifies the authors Bush and Lewis describe is the conflict within them of medieval and modern ways of thinking. Thus, as compared with Dilthey, both Bush and Lewis tend to dissolve the unity of their periods.

As a result, Bush and Lewis contextualize only in an ad hoc way. Though Hegel explained the *Geist,* spirit, or unified mentality of an age by metaphysics, and Dilthey explained it by wholly natural causes, both these authors could cite the *Geist* of a period as the context for each of its manifestations. Lacking such a unified context, Bush and Lewis could only connect whatever features of texts they happened to be interested in with whatever bits of context seemed relevant.

Theirs are literary histories in the age of criticism— the age of the massive influence of T. S. Eliot and the New Criticism. Both Bush and Lewis give an enormous amount of contextual information and explanation. They perceive literary works as part of a style, cluster, school, or tradition; or they explain them by some strand of religious, political, or other opinion in their time. Bush, moreover, defended a historical, contextual approach to literature in a controversy with Cleanth Brooks that was well known in the 1950s. Nevertheless, in writing about individual authors, both Bush and Lewis extend the genre of literary history by including more criticism than had hitherto been customary. Criticism is, of course, a term of uncertain meaning, but in this context it means an analytic, evaluative discourse that does not refer to history. Because Bush and Lewis conceived context as *Geist*, did not conceive *Geist* as unified, and gave much space to criticism, their literary histories are less contextual than many written before and since.

In *Wordsworth: The Sense of History* (1989), Alan Liu explains literary texts by political and social realities, but his conceptions are more complicated than those we have encountered hitherto.[26] A couple of examples may enable us to test Liu's long, detailed, intricate argument. Wordsworth was in France on the Fete of Federation, 14 July 1790, and witnessed, as he traveled through France with his friend Robert Jones, the enthusiasm of that moment. It is possible, says Liu, to recapture approximately the "French view" of Federation Day and to compare this with Wordsworth's view, as expressed in his autobiographical *The Prelude*.[27] Doing this, Liu finds that Wordsworth aestheticized what he saw. He viewed the political festivities in France as a spectacle, and his verse rendered them in the conventions of georgic poetry.

In another, more famous passage of *The Prelude*, written in 1804, Wordsworth celebrates the imagination rising in "strength/ Of usurpation" from the "mind's abyss" (bk. 6, lines 592–616). For several previous years, Liu observes, "'usurper' was applied to Bonaparte in English parliamentary speeches, pamphlets, and newspapers with the consistency of a technical term" (27). Other features of the passage in book 6 also recall Napoleon. For example, the lines come as Wordsworth narrates his walking tour in the Alps where Napoleon had campaigned. "A Swiss mountain pass in 1804 was first and foremost a military site" (27).

It is important to notice the concept of mediation

[26] Alan Liu, *Wordsworth: The Sense of History* (Stanford: Stanford UP, 1989).

[27] William Wordsworth, *The Prelude*, ed. Ernest de Selincourt and Helen Darbishire (Oxford: Clarendon, 1959) bk. 6, lines 342–408; see Liu 15.

underlying the second example. Liu does not go directly from the historical events concerning Napoleon to Wordsworth's poem but from the events to their representations in popular discourses; he assumes that these associated Napoleon and usurpation in Wordsworth's mind and are the context of the passage in book 6.

In both these examples, Liu argues, Wordsworth's poetry can be said to "deny history." In the one case, the Revolution is treated as happy pastoral, in the other, the imagination displaces Napoleon. The imagination treads the stage of Wordsworth's poem as a usurping "power," a type of Napoleon, but also as a criticism of Napoleon, since its usurpation is benign and reveals ultimate truth. "Wordsworth's stress in 1804 that the Imagination is its own reward, and so eschews spoils and trophies, should be seen to reject precisely Napoleon's famed spoliations" (29). Both passages in *The Prelude* illustrate the pervasive Wordsworthean theme, easily criticized as ideological, by which revolution and utopia take place, not in the political world, but in the psychic and moral life of the individual.

But, says Liu, though history is denied in Wordsworth's poetry, his texts refer to what is being denied. The paean to imagination mentions trophies and spoils. Moreover, on principles derived from structuralist thought, we can assume that what is denied is *always* present. A culture produces "reality" by laying over the amorphousness of experience a grid of concepts, thus converting "reality" into a structured field, and the whole field is implicit in any moment of it. Through historical research, we can reconstruct the different interpretive positions and emotional attitudes that could be held in a certain time toward a specific event. If Wordsworth adopts position x, positions y and z, which he does not adopt, are also present to his mind and thus are being denied in an act of conscious or unconscious will. Thus we can say not only that Wordsworth took an aesthetic view of Federation Day but also that at some level of his being he chose not to adopt the French view, and we can further speculate that his wish to deny this view was the impelling motive toward the aesthetic view.

This method of contextual interpretation and explanation Liu calls a "denied positivism able to discriminate absence" (24). That "literary texts emerge . . . precisely through a critical or second-order negation: the arbitrary but nevertheless determined differentiation by which they do *not* articulate historical contexts" (46) is, for Liu, a universal principle of literary creation. Thus Liu agrees with Wood and with Gilbert and Gubar in explaining texts by their matrix in material life, but where these assume a direct reflection, Liu perceives a deflective or oppositional relation of text to context.

Liu's argument is vulnerable to all the objections that bear on historical contextualism in general. He constructs a context and asserts that this context shaped the texts he discusses. He tries to support his assumption by circular demonstrations. Only two areas of context are foregrounded: the political and sociological, and the choice of these is again a premise or an act of faith. The method wrongly presumes that, in Wallace Stevens's phrase, a poem is "the cry of its occasion." It brings no insight into the qualitative aspects of literature. Since there can be no objective criterion of relevance, the context can be elaborated at great length, and the insight thus obtained may not be worth the effort. Liu, for example, goes for thirty pages into sociological information and analysis, with much original research pertaining to family structure and ideology in the Lake District, in order to interpret one scene in *The Borderers* (236–66). The principle of contextual explanation is used in a self-contradictory way, being applied to Wordsworth's texts but not to the texts by which Wordsworth is interpreted.

The difference between Liu and other literary historians is that he sees most of these objections. He naturally does not admit, in so many words, that by his selection and interpretation of data he constructs the context, rather than objectively discovering it, but his book has a remarkable epilogue, and in it a voice asks Liu whether "what you mean by history is distinguishable from what your poet meant by imagination?" (501). To this question neither Liu nor anyone has a satisfactory answer. We cannot deny that contexts are constructed by literary historians; we cannot concede that all constructions are equally valid; and we cannot completely agree on criteria as to which to prefer. In relating texts to historical contexts, Liu tries to achieve credibility by circularity. We may consider, for example, his argument that "in the context of the years immediately preceding 1804, 'usurper' cannot refer to anyone other than Napoleon" (26). Reading popular discourses of the time, Liu has found that Napoleon was frequently called a usurper. But he carried out this research because he guessed that usurpation meant Napoleon; he even wanted it to do so, and his research confirmed his wish. He has not tested other hypotheses; in other words, he has not tried to explain Wordsworth's metaphor of usurpation through different contexts. Generalizing, we may say that, since as contextual interpreters we cannot explore more than a small area of context, we can never be sure that it is the most relevant area.

Liu's argument violates its contextualist premises. In this type of historical explanation, any strand of context may become an event to be contextualized and logically must become this if the explanation is carried out in further detail. To explain fully why a metaphor of usurpation in Wordsworth's poetry may be interpreted as an allusion to Napoleon, one would have to contextualize the context of Wordsworth's expression. In other words, one would have to explain contextually why Pitt, Sheridan, Coleridge, and others referred to Napoleon as a usurper in political speeches, pamphlets, and newspaper articles. The distinction between event and context is not intrinsic, but conventional and practical, the event being the portion of the context that one foregrounds and tries to explain. We cannot, therefore, allow two different rules of interpretation, one for the contextualized events and one for the strands of context. Yet Liu does this. Literary texts deflect their context, he argues, but he takes for granted that other discourses, which are the contexts of literature, respond directly to their contexts. If Liu assumed that all texts, literary and otherwise, deflected their contexts, he would find it very much more difficult to establish a context.

In Stephen Greenblatt's *Shakespearean Negotiations* the arbitrary choice of context, inherent in all historical contextualizing, becomes obvious and extreme.[28] In each essay Greenblatt picks out a particular discourse produced in Shakespeare's time, such as Thomas Harriot's *A Brief and True Report of the New Found Land of Virginia* (1588) or Samuel Harsnett's *A Declaration of Egregious Popish Impostures* (1603). These discourses, or some features of them, are described at length, set in a context of other discourses on similar topics, and interpreted according to ideas drawn from Foucault, from neo-Marxist thought, and from cultural anthropology. Each of Greenblatt's essays brings one of these discourses, thus richly saturated, into relation with one or more of Shakespeare's plays.

This procedure is very peculiar, or it would seem so had it not been so widely imitated. Every other contextual interpreter I have cited assumes that the textual features he or she discusses were determined or partly determined by the context exhibited. Greenblatt makes no such assumption. The discourses he describes contributed either little or nothing at all to the genesis of the plays. Greenblatt does not even attempt, usually, to trace a path of mediations between the other discourse and Shakespeare's play. To show that Shakespeare was aware

---

[28] Alan Liu strongly emphasizes the arbitrary choice of context in Historicism in "The Power of Formalism: The New Historicism," *ELH* 56 (Winter 1989): 722.

of the other discourse is not necessary to his argument. Moreover, Greenblatt did not himself need to read these other discourses in order to produce his interpretations of Shakespeare, and Greenblatt's readers would not need to be instructed about these other discourses in order to follow his interpretations. Thus the context is made intensely interesting and expressive in itself, but its relation to Shakespeare is ancillary. A harsh criticism might be that it was ornamental.

I begin with the question of mediation. Robert Wood assumes that Homer saw what he describes. Dilthey shows that Novalis had read the works that determined his own. Alan Liu is careful to trace the paths from Napoleon's doings to representations of them in newspapers and thence to Wordsworth's consciousness. Greenblatt points out that Shakespeare had read Harsnett's work on exorcisms, but this is only incidental to his argument. Discourses, he says, are made from collectively produced materials—words, myths, customs. They are made within social institutions and are partly determined by the aims of the institution. Between discourses, or between the various institutions of Elizabethan society, there was a circulation, such that each one appropriated, reinterpreted, and applied to its own purposes materials from other "culturally demarcated zone[s]."[29] Particular instances of exchange between cultural zones and discourses may be called *transactions* or *negotiations.*

Mediation takes place not at the individual level but at the cultural level, in the anthropological conception of culture. Yet Greenblatt does not posit an organic, totally unified culture about which one could write a master narrative. His concepts of circulation and negotiation between cultural institutions are designed to secure a continuity between different discourses, making it fruitful to read them together and, yet, to also preserve their dif-

[29] Stephen Greenblatt, *Shakespearean Negotiations* (Oxford: Clarendon, 1988) 7.

ferences and oppositions. Because of the circulation between cultural zones, any discourse can be brought into
conjunction with any other, so long, that is, as the essayist can construct an interrelation between them. But no
one has yet written a New Historicist essay on discourses
between which no connection could be found. By the
usual circular logic, in other words, the result demon-
strates the usefulness of the method.

But is it useful? If we view Greenblatt's essays as
interpretations—and very interesting ones—of Shakespeare's plays, we find that the contextualization, the
exhibition of Harriot's discourse, or Harsnett's polemic,
or Hugh Latimer's sermon, contributes very little to clarify or support Greenblatt's readings of Shakespeare. Greenblatt says that he uses Harriot's discourse on the land of
Virginia as an "interpretive model" for understanding the
far more complex "relation between orthodoxy and sub-
version" in Shakespeare's history plays (23). But if we ask
by what model does Greenblatt interpret Harriot, the
answer is by a set of ideas that he brings to Harriot, brings
also to the history plays, and would anyway have brought
to the plays whether he had read Harriot or not.

Samuel Harsnett's polemic describes the exorcism of
demons as a fraud. Such cases, Harsnett says, are really
only theater, only illusion. Both the persons supposedly
possessed by a demon and the officiating clergy are
merely staging performances, and the credulous who believe that they witness the expulsion of a demon are
gulled. Since both the Jesuits and the Puritan preachers
conducted exorcisms, Harsnett promotes the Anglican
church by denying the claim of its rivals to operate this
spiritual power.

When, in *King Lear*, Edgar acts the role of a demoniac,
the play reiterates Harsnett's line. Mad Tom is not possessed by a demon but is only Edgar playing a role. But as
King Lear takes this understanding from the Anglican
church, it is *"emptied out"* (119). As Harsnett undermines
exorcisms, he does not wish to deny the reality of super-

natural evil. But in *Lear*, the fact that demonic possession is only feigned becomes one strand in a much larger
web of implication. "In Shakespeare, the realization that
demonic possession is theatrical imposture leads not to a
clarification — the clear-eyed satisfaction of the man who
refuses to be gulled — but to a deeper uncertainty, a loss of
moorings, in the face of evil" (122). The suggestion,
which Greenblatt supports with several references to the
text, is that *Lear* entertains the possibility of a world in
which neither evil nor good has supernatural meaning, in
which man's moral life has no transcendent dimension,
and the evil presented in the play is merely natural. Such
is Greenblatt's argument, lamentably shorn in this synop-
sis of its richness, subtlety, and suggestiveness.

My point is that Greenblatt's interpretation of *Lear* is
based simply on his reading of the text; more exactly,
with a wonderful critical pathos it projects his own beliefs into the text. What relation does it have to Harsnett?
At most, Greenblatt could claim only that reading Harsnett contributed very slightly to the "uncertainty, a loss
of moorings, in the face of evil" of *King Lear*, but even
this interpretation of the impact of reading Harsnett depends on Greenblatt's prior, more general interpretation
of *Lear*. Greenblatt developed this interpretation for reasons that had nothing to do with Harsnett.

Perhaps this is only to say that Greenblatt's essay is
not really a contextual explanation or interpretation of
Lear. His essay combines two intentions that are logically separate: to interpret the play and to exemplify the
processes of circulation and negotiation among cultural
discourses and institutions. Harsnett is seriously relevant only to the latter topic, for which he provides a brilliant illustration. I wish to make it clear that in discussing Greenblatt's and other literary histories, my object of
criticism has not been these particular writers but the
contextual method. The examples I have chosen are
justly admired. Neither am I immune to the plausibility
and fascination of contextual explanation at its best, and

I am perfectly aware that other modes of explanation and interpretation are equally vulnerable to fundamental critiques. Nevertheless, if one wishes to practice as, say, a New Historicist, the aporias of other schools of criticism should not console for one's own.

7

Theories of Immanent Change

LITERATURE, SAYS BRUNETIÈRE, HAS "IN ITSELF and from the first the sufficient principle of its development."[1] This is the essential assumption of an immanent or internal explanation of the literary series. "A poem," Harold Bloom maintains, is the *"rewriting"* of a previous poem; "one poem helps to form another."[2] "The form of the work of art," Viktor Shklovsky argues, "is determined by its relation to other, already existing forms";[3] and as the Russian Formalists elaborate this insight, the literary series is conceived as changing by its own inherent dynamic.

The system is not completely independent of happenings that are external to literature, but the immanent factors are far more important. Bloom also concedes that "even the strongest poets are subject to influences not poetical" but nowhere talks about such influences.[4] And

[1] Ferdinand Brunetière, *Etudes critiques sur l'histoire de la littérature française* (Paris: Hachette, 1912) 3, quoted in René Wellek, *A History of Modern Criticism 1750–1950* (New Haven: Yale UP, 1965) 4:65.

[2] Harold Bloom, *Poetry and Repression* (New Haven: Yale UP, 1976) 3, and *Poetics of Influence*, ed. John Hollander (New Haven: Henry R. Schwab, 1988) 47.

[3] Viktor Shklovsky, "The Connections between the Devices of Plot Construction and Stylistic Devices in General," in *Texte der russischen Formalisten*, vol. 1, *Texte zur allgemeinen Literaturtheorie und zur Theorie der Prosa*, ed. Jurij Striedter (Munich: Wilhelm Fink, 1969) 51.

[4] Harold Bloom, *The Anxiety of Influence: A Theory of Poetry* (New York: Oxford UP, 1973) 11.

Brunetière acknowledges that the point of view of Taine and his disciples, who interpret literature as a product of historical and sociological realities—of race, moment, and milieu, in Taine's triad—cannot be completely rejected: "I have not omitted to note those other influences on which it is the habit to lay weight, the influence of race or the influence of environment." But Brunetière continues, in a passage Shklovsky quotes in 1916: "However, as I hold that of all the influences which make themselves felt in the history of a literature, the principle is that of *works on works*, I have made it my special concern to trace this influence and to follow its continuous action."[5]

Brunetière perfectly understood the advantages of an immanent literary history. When we explain the literary series by external circumstances or events, our construction may be heterogeneous, miscellaneous, a bird's nest of straw, string, twigs, grass, and feathers—whatever we happened to find. We foreground now one bit of context, now another, and the second may have no relation to the first except that both contributed to the literary event. No context can be fully described, no explanation can seem complete. Both intellectually and aesthetically, such literary histories must be inelegant.

An immanent literary history is still contextual; it puts an author or text in a supposedly determining context of other authors or texts. But since it drastically limits the area of context, it enables us to create relatively coherent literary histories, focused and interrelated narratives. For example, without referring to medieval social structures, politics, or *Geistesgeschichte*, Brunetière would trace how the *Romans d'aventures* (*Amadis*) evolved from the *Chanson de geste* (*Roland*) by a gradual differentiating of functions. The *Chanson de geste* is "almost history." But from it the genres of memoir and

---

[5] Ferdinand Brunetière, *Manual of the History of French Literature*, trans. Ralph Derechef (London: T. Fisher Unwin, 1898) vii.

chronicle detached themselves, and "in the degree that it lightened itself of its historical substance, the heroic poem gave a more considerable part of itself to legend and dream; this is the epoch of the *Tales of the Round Table*," and led to such works as *Amadis*, in which "improbability is the principal beauty. They are written to give liberty to the imagination in full career."[6]

In order to earn its narrative coherence, a theory of immanent explanation must answer three questions. It must say why literature is determined more by immanent than by external factors. It must explain the superficially puzzling fact that works differ from the works that supposedly formed them. And it must account for the particular character or direction of the difference.

There are a great many quasi-immanent explanations of literary change, and we may ignore most of them. They are no longer plausible. We may, for example, exclude all cyclical theories, such as Wilhelm Scherer's theory that German literature reaches a high point every six hundred years (600, 1200, 1800); W. B. Yeats's wheel of culture through the twenty-eight phases of the moon; and Northrop Frye's rotation of modes from myth to irony and over again.[7] Excluded also are theories that interpret the literary series by analogies to natural life and death, the drearily familiar figures of the birth, maturity, decline, and end of a form, genre, national literature, and so on. When they are intended as explanations, these flowers of rhetoric are inappropriate, for whatever else it may resemble, the literary series is not like a plant or animal. Behind this analogy lies, very often, the notion of a *Geist* as the subject going through the organic cycle — the *Geist* of tragedy, or the *Geist* of Russian literature. Probably a *Geist*

[6] Ferdinand Brunetière, *L'Evolution des genres dans l'histoire de la littérature* (Paris: Hachette, 1914) 5–6.

[7] Wilhelm Scherer, *Geschichte der Deutschen Litteratur*, 10th ed. (Berlin: Weidmann, 1905) 18–22; W. B. Yeats, *A Vision* (New York: Macmillan, 1956) 67–184; Northrop Frye, *Anatomy of Criticism: Four Essays* (Princeton: Princeton UP, 1957) 33–35, 42.

is what Friedrich Schlegel had in mind when he said that Greek culture was "completely original and national, a whole complete in itself, which through merely inner development reached a highest point, and in a complete circle sank back again into itself."[8] The thought of *Geist* recalls Hegel and the many explanations, still put forward today, of the history of a movement, genre, and so on, as the logical (dialectical) development of an idea. I have earlier expressed skepticism about such correlations of the contingencies of history with logic.

Theories that present the historical changes of literature as an oscillation between two poles also have little to recommend them.[9] The idea that literature alternates between phases of convention and revolt was given prominence by John Livingston Lowes,[10] but occurs in many variant formulations. Such schemes are supposedly derived from study of literary history, but are actually a priori conceptions based on analogies. Occasionally such antitheses have been modeled on Wölfflin's description as an art historian of two opposed modes of perception, the "Renaissance," or linear, and the "Baroque," or "painterly," but even Wölfflin had great difficulty in applying his scheme to explain the history of art. For when he lined up paintings in a series, he saw transition rather than clearly demarcated, polar types, and his memorable confession deserves to be quoted again: "Everything is transition and it is hard to answer the man who regards history as an endless flow. For us, intellectual self-preservation demands that we should classify the infinity of events with reference to a few results."[11] T. E. Hulme,

[8] Friedrich Schlegel, "Über das Studium der griechischen Poesie" (1795), in *Kritische Ausgabe*, ed. Ernst Behler et al. (Paderborn: F. Schöningh, 1979) 1:302.

[9] On this subject see Elémer Hankiss, "The Structure of Literary Evolution," *Poetics* no. 5 (1972).

[10] John Livingston Lowes, *Convention and Revolt in Poetry* (Boston: Houghton Mifflin, 1919).

[11] Heinrich Wölfflin, *Principles of Art History: The Problem of*

Fritz Strich, and Louis Cazamian may be cited among the many persons who have tried to base literary history on a typology of the romantic and the classical, literature swinging periodically from one pole to the other.

We may also, in this context, pay no attention to theories of the necessary progress or decline of literature. The notion that forms gradually and progressively exhaust their possibilities, and that this process determines their evolution, is untestable, since we can never specify in advance what the possibilities of a form may be, and we can never say, at any point in time, that they are played out.[12] No theory could be more brilliantly and variously expounded than was, in the eighteenth and nineteenth centuries, the idea that the arts and literature decline as civilization advances.[13] But this theory of decline is invalidated, at least in my opinion, by the literature produced since. Neither is the literary series teleological. It is not, for example, impelled by a technical aim that continues through generations and is gradually achieved, like the effort for realistic illusion that, according to E. H. Gombrich, governs the development of painting into the nineteenth century.[14]

We observed that theorists of immanent literary change generally concede that external factors also play a role. Often it is difficult to know whether a theory should be considered immanent or not. The cyclical theory of Scherer, for example, is an immanent one because it posits a regular, periodic recurrence of literary flowerings and witherings. On the other hand, it gives no reason for this periodicity, which might be due to chance;

Development of Style in Later Art, trans. M. D. Hottinger (New York: Dover, 1950) 227.

[12] Compare John Frow, *Marxism and Literary History* (Cambridge: Harvard UP, 1986) 110–11.

[13] Judith Plotz, *Ideas of the Decline of Poetry: A Study in English Criticism from 1700 to 1830* (New York: Garland, 1987).

[14] E. H. Gombrich, *Art and Illusion: A Study in the Psychology of Pictorial Representation* (New York: Pantheon, 1960).

and Scherer's might even be a contextual explanation insofar as it correlates these flowerings with German openness to foreign influences and with ideal social attitudes about women. A *Geist* is usually described as a totality in which literature is an organic part. The same principle that pervades the totality (e.g., Greek culture) works also in literature and produces its continual transition. Such organic theories of literary development are both immanent and contextual.

The theory of Wölfflin is immanent because he argues that "the effect of picture on picture as a factor in style is much more important than what comes directly from the imitation of nature," and because two "forms of apperception" express themselves in alternation throughout the history of painting. On the other hand, if we ask why the reversals occur when they do, why the painterly replaces the linear style (or vice versa) at a given moment, Wölfflin hesitates between immanent and external explanations. "Here we encounter the great problem—is the change in the forms of apprehension the result of an inward development . . . or is it an impulse from outside . . . which determines the change." Both answers are possible.

> Certainly we must not imagine that an internal mechanism runs automatically and produces, in any conditions, the said series of forms of apprehension. . . . But the human imaginative faculty will always make its organization and possibilities of development felt in the history of art. It is true, we only see what we look for, but we only look for what we can see. Doubtless certain forms of beholding pre-exist as possibilities; whether and how they come to development depends on outward circumstances. (230)

On the whole, Wölfflin believes that the painterly style develops out of the linear by immanent principles, but that in the other reversal, the return from the painterly to the linear, the main impetus lies certainly in outward circumstances (230–33).

A major theory of decline in the eighteenth century attributed literature's dwindling imagination and passion to increasingly refined manners, civilized rationality, the growth of literary criticism, and the greater abstraction of language as it matures, that is, to causes external to literature itself; hence, this explanation might be considered contextual rather than immanent. But literature, according to this theory, has an essential role in creating the social conditions that cause its decline. Thus the relation of external and immanent causes may be dialectical. An external factor becomes internal if it enters literature and changes it. If an immanent transformation of literature has an effect in the social world, this effect becomes a factor external to literature and may have an impact on it, thus becoming internal again.[15] The distinction of external and internal factors is not meaningless, but it can be made only with regard to a particular literary event at a moment in time.

Only three immanent theories have any degree of plausibility and practical impact on the writing of literary history at the present time. They are the theories of the Russian Formalists, of W. J. Bate about the remorselessly growing "burden of the past," and of Harold Bloom. I also note the theories of Brunetière, for though he has now no influence and hardly any readers, he was the first to express the necessity and the possibility of immanent explanation of the type now current. In fact, he adumbrated some of the central ideas of the Russian Formalists.

Since Formalism was a dialogic critical movement, involving several thinkers and changing positions over thirteen years, and is extended in Czech Structuralism, it is misleading to speak of a single Formalist theory of literary history. Therefore, I will focus on magnificent

---

[15] For discussion of this point, see M. M. Bakhtin/P. M. Medvedev, *The Formal Method in Literary Scholarship: A Critical Introduction to Sociological Poetics*, trans. Albert J. Wehrle (Cambridge: Harvard UP, 1985) 26–30.

essays by Yury Tynyanov on "The Literary Fact" and "Literary Evolution," though with some reference to earlier Formalist writings. First, however, I note the remarkable agreement in essential points of all these theories.

None of these theorists spend much time arguing their primary assumption that immanent factors are the decisive ones. They hope, no doubt, to establish this concretely, by showing the importance of immanent factors in particular cases and by uncovering the mechanisms by which they determine literary works. There are repeated claims that these immanent explanations are grounded, more than other explanations, in the actual psychology of writers, in their conscious and unconscious perceptions and intentions during the creative process. Thus these immanent theories are unhistorical, for they are based on something—the psychology of writers—that is assumed to be unchanging from age to age.

All that changes, according to these theories, is the past itself, growing more oppressive as it accumulates, and therefore mobilizing psychological defenses more intensely. As Bloom puts it, the anxiety of influence "has increased as history proceeds"; it "is strongest where poetry is most lyrical, most subjective, and stemming directly from the personality."[16] Poets and novelists have often testified that these theories express dilemmas they actually feel. Yet we shall see that the principle by which these theories explain the course of modern literature is said to operate in some writers, but not in all.

This is not really a defect of the theories, for individuality is a stumbling block in any theoretical explanation of literary history. Since the explanatory principle does not apply to all writers in the same way, a second principle is required to explain why certain writers were subject to the first principle and others were less so or not at all. Why, in Bloom's terms, are some but not all writers "strong"? Or why, in the terms of the Russian Formalists,

---

[16] Bloom, The Anxiety of Influence 62.

do some writers produce automatized works and others defamiliarized ones? If individuality is unexplainable and makes a difference, no theory, either contextual or immanent, can completely explain literary history. Theorists of literary history must allow for the effects of individuality in order to be plausible, but for the sake of a general explanation they must downplay the role of individuality as much as possible. They must assume that, as Keats put it, even "the mightiest Minds" are subdued "to the service of the time being."[17] To the extent that writers are not thus subdued, literary histories can be no more than suites of biographies, which is what they often have been.

These immanent theories all posit essentially the same principle of literary change: the desire or necessity of writers to produce works unlike those of previous writers.[18] There is, as Brunetière says, "nothing metaphysical" about it: "We wish to be different from those who have preceded us in history: this design is the origin and determining cause of changes of taste as of literary revolutions."[19] He does not say why we wish to be different, but innumerable reasons suggest themselves, ranging from the need of an artist to be noticed to dissatisfaction with a currently dominant style.

H. P. H. Teesing quotes Spranger's *Psychologie des Jugendalters* on this point: "The ready and formed

[17] John Keats to Reynolds, 3 May 1818, *The Letters of John Keats, 1814–1821*, ed. Hyder E. Rollins (Cambridge: Harvard UP, 1958) 1:282.

[18] Colin Martindale, *Romantic Progression: The Psychology of Literary Change* (Washington, D.C.: Hemisphere, 1975), develops a similar argument from the point of view of a sociologist. He describes the vicious circle of the autonomy of poetry. A work of art must be different from previous productions. As the autonomy of a poetic subculture increases, fewer social constraints limit the expression of originality. "The poet experiences a stronger pressure toward novelty and his audience exerts a lessened resistance to it . . . but these changes make poetry less palatable to the audience and thus lead to further increments in autonomy" (11, 51).

[19] Brunetière, *Manual* vii.

(Ranke says: 'the life found before one') is . . . accepted as obvious. . . . The accent of life places itself on what one lacks, on the places that have remained empty in the inner and in the shared world."[20] Or we might note that every style suppresses certain aspects of reality, while foregrounding others, and its limitations become apparent over time. When the style seems a stylization only, it will be abandoned in a literary culture that values mimesis. In the Russian Formalist model, literature proceeds dialectically through moments of automatization and defamiliarization. The purpose of art, says Shklovsky, is "to increase the difficulty and length of perception,"[21] to make perception fuller and more vivid. What the techniques of art make perceptible are both the art itself and also the things represented within it. "The material of the work of art," Shklovsky says elsewhere, "is constantly played with the pedal, that is, it is rendered prominent, 'made to resound.'"[22] Thus, when themes and techniques have become familiar, banal, and automatized, art no longer has its effect, and a different principle of construction must develop. The new principle of construction announces itself, is applied to the greatest possible number of different phenomena, and in turn, Tynyanov explains, becomes "automatised and calls forth opposed principles of construction." "If there are epochs in which all poets write 'well,' then the 'bad' poet is the genius."[23]

In Bate's theory, past literature constitutes, for writers, a canon of the forbidden, of forms that can no longer be used because they have already been fully exploited. He

---

[20] H. P. H. Teesing, *Das Problem der Perioden in der Literaturgeschichte* (Groningen: J. B. Wolters, 1949) 65–66.

[21] Viktor Shklovsky, "Art as Technique," in *Russian Formalist Criticism: Four Essays*, trans. Lee T. Lemon and Marion J. Reis (Lincoln: U of Nebraska P, 1965) 12.

[22] Shklovsky, "The Connections between the Devices of Plot Construction" 51.

[23] Yury Tynyanov, "The Literary Fact," in *Texte der russischen Formalisten* 1:413, 403.

quotes T. S. Eliot: "Not only every great poet, but every genuine, though lesser poet, fulfills once for all some possibility of the language, and so leaves one possibility less for his successors"; and "When a great poet has lived, certain things have been done once for all, and cannot be achieved again."[24] As the past grows longer, it engenders in writers an intensifying crisis of self-confidence, a "deepening of self-consciousness" (4), powerfully affecting what and how they write.

Yet, our theorists concede that many writers do not wish to be different. There are the works in automatized styles of which the Formalists speak, the poets of generosity of spirit, in Bloom's generous description of them, who are directly open to predecessors.[25] Only Bate has no need to admit exceptions to the universally working principle of immanent change. But the point is that the exceptions are not important. As Brunetière put it, "There have also been writers who have wished to do 'the same thing' as their predecessors. I am well aware of the fact! But in the history of literature and of art, they are precisely the writers who *do not count*."[26] They do not count because literary histories are narratives of change; therefore, the works in which change is hardly visible must fall out of them.

But also such writers lack merit and do not count qualitatively. "After much observation," Bloom concludes that "where generosity is involved, the poets influenced are minor or weaker; the more generosity . . . the poorer the poets involved."[27] Even more than other literary historians, immanent ones are strongly tempted to identify literary excellence with conspicuous novelty in technique or subject matter. This identification has often been brought as a reproach against the Russian Formal-

---

[24] W. Jackson Bate, *The Burden of the Past and the English Poet* (Cambridge: Harvard UP, 1970) 4, 122.

[25] Bloom, *Poetics of Influence* 82.

[26] Brunetière, *Manual* vii, fn.; my italics.

[27] Bloom, *Poetics of Influence* 83.

ists. Their critics argue that there is no necessary connection between defamiliarized form and literary excellence. Great works may be quite traditional in method and content and experimental ones may be trivial.[28]

The major criticism of these immanent explanations has been that they are immanent; in other words, they isolate the development of literature from concrete, sociopolitical conditions. "Fundamental shifts in literary tradition," to quote Jurij Striedter, often "cannot be explained except as responses to definite extraliterary situations."[29] Marxist critics, such as Peter Medvedev and Kurt Konrad, make this argument, and so do sympathetic critics such as Striedter (70–75), Jauss, Erlich, and Frow (94).[30] We need not elaborate the criticism here, but it is interesting that immanent theories have themselves been explained as products of a historical context, both by the Formalists themselves and by their antagonists.[31]

According to some Marxist opponents, the Formalists project the modernist alienation of the artist from society, itself a reflection of the class obsolescence of the bourgeois artist, as a theory of literary history. Or the argument might be cast in different terms: immanent theories, historically considered, are a product of social and economic developments that compelled art either to become a commodity or to move into the marginal posi-

---

[28] See René Wellek, "The Fall of Literary History," in *The Attack on Literature and Other Essays* (Chapel Hill: U of North Carolina P, 1982) 74.

[29] Jurij Striedter, *Literary Structure, Evolution, and Value: Russian Formalism and Czech Structuralism Reconsidered* (Cambridge: Harvard UP, 1989) 73. The essay I quote, "The Formalist Theory of Prose and Literary Evolution," is reprinted from vol. 1, *Texte der russischen Formalisten* lxxiv.

[30] The views of Konrad are summarized in Striedter 115–16; those of other Marxist critics of the Formalists in Victor Erlich, *Russian Formalism: History-Doctrine*, 3d. ed. (New Haven: Yale UP, 1965); see also Erlich 198; and H. R. Jauss, *Toward an Aesthetic of Reception*, trans. Timothy Bahti (Minneapolis: U of Minnesota P, 1982) 18, 107.

[31] Boris Eikhenbaum, "The Literary Life," in *Texte der russischen Formalisten* 1:465. For discussion see Frow 116.

tions, in relation to society, of soi-disant autonomy or opposition. Immanent explanations assume that the autonomy of art, which modern artists claim, is really the case.

By the Formalist theory alone, one cannot explain the direction of literary change.[32] Bate and Bloom are less exposed to this criticism. Bate sees in modern literature a progressive "retrenchment" toward "refinement, nuance, indirection, and finally, through the continued pressure for difference, into the various forms of anti-art" (10). Bloom, who is more deterministic, envisions a vague, necessary "diminishment of poetry."[33] By the Formalist theories, only two different principles of construction would be required through all time. As one became automatized, the other would announce itself, and when it in turn was automatized, the previous one would again emerge. To account for the enormous number of principles of construction that have actually appeared, additional explanation is needed, and the Formalist theory cannot provide it.[34]

These immanent explanations depend on questionable assumptions about the psychology of writers. Moreover, the Formalists and Bloom assume that persons who are not writers may and should read as writers do, thus expanding their theories of literary history into theories about reading. Bloom's various books are more directly on this subject than on literary influence or history. Only Bate makes crystal clear that he distinguishes between the mental acts and preoccupations of writers as they read and

[32] The point is made by Yury Tynyanov and Roman Jakobson in "Problems in the Study of Literature and Language" (1928): to explain the actual path of literary change when several paths are open, there must be "an analysis of the correlations between the literary series and other historical series." *Readings in Russian Poetics: Formalist and Structuralist Views*, ed. Ladislav Matejka and Krystna Pomorska (Cambridge: MIT P, 1971) 81.

[33] Bloom, *The Anxiety of Influence* 10.

[34] Compare Bakhtin/Medvedev 163.

those of ordinary persons (22–23). Whether writers actually do read in the ways described can only be surmised.

The theories of reading put forward by the Russian Formalists and Bloom are normative rather than descriptive. They imagine the act of reading as it ought to be among writers, critics, and a certain, indefinite segment of other readers—those, namely, who are capable of the processes described. Literature, the argument goes, is created and must be read in relation to other literature. The literature of any time, says Tynyanov, forms a synchronic system in which all elements are correlated and affect each other reciprocally, and "there can be no investigation of literary phenomena outside of their interrelationships."[35] That a fact exists as a *literary* fact depends on its differential quality, as Tynyanov says (441), and this is apparent only when it is viewed within the system that produced it. A poem, Bloom argues, is engendered by a parent poem.

The reader, then, must acquire an objectively accurate awareness of the system of literature as it was when the work was created. Since it is assumed that the writer possessed this awareness, we can simply say that the reader must see the system or the parent poem as the writer saw it. The function and aesthetic achievement of a work cannot be understood if the work is placed in some other context or considered in isolation. Presumably the ignorant may be allowed their enjoyments of literature, but their responses have, by these theories, no importance. When I had not yet read many poems, all were different or defamiliarized, which is perhaps why I loved them all. Ignorance is bliss. Since this was puberty, I was especially stirred by love poems, which shows that we intensely perceive not only what is different but, even more, what we are interested in.[36]

---

[35] Yury Tynyanov, "On Literary Evolution," in *Texte der russischen Formalisten* 1:447.

[36] Compare Bakhtin/Medvedev 156.

Though immanent explanations require that we adopt the point of view of writers, this is not always possible or especially desirable. If the Formalists and Bloom correctly described the sort of reading we must do in order to explain literary history, they would still be wrong in generalizing their theories into prescriptions for reading in general.

For these theorists, the principle of literary change is not only the need of writers to be different but also their active rejection of predecessors. Literary succession takes place with and by means of antagonism and strife. Previous works are in some sense a threat, Bate observes, both practically to our possibilities of productivity and psychologically to our self-esteem. Though Bate does not emphasize this, it is implicit in his thought that the latecomer may feel the Nietzschean *ressentiment* of the anxious toward the free. If a certain style—this is Tynyanov's way of putting it—has become dominant, it will be attacked. "We can speak of succession by inheritance," Tynyanov says, "only with the appearance of a school, of epigones, but not with the phenomena of literary evolution, the principle of which is strife and succession."[37] For Bloom, the principle of literary change lies in the oedipal struggle of poets with predecessors as fathers. A poet creates a poem by misunderstanding the poem of a predecessor. This "misprision" of the "parent poem" may be conscious or unconscious, but, in some sense, it is willful. It is necessary to the creation of the new poem and partly determines its form and content.

Even Brunetière, though a nineteenth-century critic, could perceive literary history as conflict. Led by his analogy of literary history to Darwinian evolution, he speculated, in phrases that must have been suggestive to the Formalists, that genres compete with each other like natural species, one taking over subject matter that had belonged to a different genre, or one displacing another in

[37] Tynyanov, "The Literary Fact" 401.

the hierarchy of genres. "If it is true that the struggle for life is never more bitter than between neighboring species, do not a host of examples offer themselves to remind us that it is not otherwise in the history of literature and of art."[38]

Difference, strife, and the third element is discontinuity. Literary evolution, for these theorists, takes place by jumps. It is not evolution, Tynyanov says, "but displacement."[39] "Poetry must leap," Bloom echoes, "it must locate itself in a discontinuous universe. . . . Discontinuity is freedom."[40] The position reverses traditional assumptions. In the nineteenth century, literary historians traced continuous transition within an organic, evolving whole or, at least, a development in which one phase prepares and leads to the next. They emphasized that a writer or a work is born in a milieu that conditions and forms. Before a work is created, its horizon of possibility is already limited, its structure and mentality partly determined, for it evolves directly from what already exists. Our theorists concede this. "What happens," says Bloom, "if one tries to write, or to teach, or to think, or even to read without the sense of tradition? Why, nothing at all happens. . . . You cannot write or teach or think or even read without imitation."[41] Which is to say that in every new work there is continuity as well as difference from past literary works. As literary historians, we emphasize one or the other, but what we emphasize is a personal choice, expressing our own values, not anything objectively knowable about the historical process.

To emphasize strife and discontinuity defamiliarizes literary history. This, in fact, is the second major advantage of immanent explanations. They promote narrative coherence and additionally, for our generation, they bring

[38] Brunetière, L'Evolution des genres 22.
[39] Tynyanov, "The Literary Fact" 395.
[40] Bloom, Poetics of Influence 96.
[41] Harold Bloom, A Map of Misreading (New York: Oxford UP, 1975) 32.

phenomena into view that have not been sufficiently perceived. To Bate, for example, we owe a new emphasis on the importance, for understanding literary change, of grasping the point of view of writers, especially the problems created for them by the mountain of past works. From Bloom comes the additional, fruitful reminder that poetic influence takes place not by reading but by misreading, by "misprision" or misunderstanding the texts of the past. These, I think, are permanent additions to the nexus of ideas by which the course of literary change can be explained. And though Bloom unnecessarily limits the concept of influence to only those relations with other poets that involve conflict, he has called attention to the variety of these struggles and of their outcomes.

The Russian Formalists contribute their clear recognition that there can be no definition of literature as such that is valid for all epochs.[42] What is considered to be literature depends on time and place. The intimate letter is a literary genre in some epochs, but in others it falls into the realm of private life outside of literature.[43] Tynyanov argues that the literature of any time is a synchronic system and that over time systems succeed each other. (This argument is opposed in postmodern emphases on the anomalous and heterogeneous in any moment of literary history.) Some elements of a system may reappear in its successor; others may not. The same form may have an altered function in the context or system of a different epoch. In the age of Spenser, the romance has a cognitive and ethical function, and is close to epic. In the age of William Morris, its function is escapist; the functions it fulfilled for Spenser are assigned to other genres.

---

[42] Compare Roland Barthes, *Critical Essays*, trans. Richard Howard (Evanston: Northwestern UP, 1972) 250–51: "History tells us that there is no such thing as a timeless essence of literature, but under the rubric of 'literature' . . . a process of very different forms, functions, institutions, reasons, and projects whose relativity it is precisely the historian's responsibility to discern."

[43] Tynyanov, "The Literary Fact" 417–23.

The proper subject of literary history is not the succession of works but the succession of systems, for to describe the work without describing the system in which it functions is meaningless. When an element of a system changes, or the function of an element, the whole system changes correlatively. Succession, therefore, is discontinuous; a system takes the place of the previous one.[44] When this happens, not only the marginal elements of the system but also the central ones may have altered; the previously central elements may move to the margin or disappear altogether. Epic and dramatic tragedy exemplify genres central to literary systems that have now vanished.

According to Tynyanov, genres are the elements of literary systems and are themselves also systems whose elements and their functions change over time. Meter was once the defining characteristic of poetry, the criterion by which the genre of poetry was distinguished from prose. In the age of free verse, meter is no longer a central element and no longer serves the same functions.[45] The literary system of a given time is not one in which all elements interact as equals. Rather, some are dominant, and others are deformed by this dominance.[46] For example, in England, the lyric was the dominant genre in the early nineteenth century. Hence the lyrical ballads, lyrical dramas (such as Shelley's *Prometheus Unbound*), and lyrical novels of that age; the pull of the dominant genre affected the others.[47] So also within genres. When meter (including rhyme) was the dominant element of poetry, the other elements were subordinated. One sees this in the poetry of the age of Tennyson, which perpetually sacrifices diction and syntax to the necessities of meter. One genre displaces another in the position of domi-

[44] Ibid. 395–97.

[45] Tynyanov, "On Literary Evolution" 441–43.

[46] Ibid. 451.

[47] Clifford Siskin, *The Historicity of Romantic Discourse* (New York: Oxford UP, 1988), has investigated some aspects of this phenomenon for the English romantic period.

nance and so, also, within genres, with their elements. In most novels the description of landscape has connecting or retarding functions; in some epochs, however, it might be the motivation for the novels. In this case, the plots would be designed to secure occasions for landscape description.[48]

When a technique becomes automatized, the genre must change. Either a familiar technique acquires a new function, or the correlation (dominance) of elements alters,[49] or new elements are incorporated, or an entirely new construction is made out of old and new elements. Often the successor genre adopts and combines elements from the "backyards and lowlands" of literature or from the speech materials of extraliterary existence.[50]

Obviously there is contradiction between the concepts of automatization and of discontinuity, since automatization and defamiliarization are represented as processes taking place within literary systems. What will eventually be welcomed as defamiliarization may at first be perceived within the current system as error, as an illegitimate departure from norms.

In other words, though Tynyanov initially denied continuous transition between systems, he admitted it within them. A year later, however, in eight theses written jointly with Roman Jakobson, he overcame this contradiction: "The opposition between synchrony and diachrony was an opposition between the concept of system and the concept of evolution; thus it loses its importance in principle as soon as we recognize that every system necessarily exists as an evolution, whereas, on the other hand, evolution is inescapably of a systemic

[48] Tynyanov, "On Literary Evolution" 443.

[49] This idea was anticipated by Ferdinand Brunetière in *L'Evolution de la poésie lyrique en France aux dix-neuvième siècle,* 10th ed. (Paris: Hachette, n.d.) 2:288: development is "the new disposition of identical elements; a 'change of front' . . . a modification of the relations which keep the parts of the same whole together."

[50] Tynyanov, "The Literary Fact" 399.

nature."[51] Though systems are synchronic, they are in process, never static. But, the assumption of discontinuity justifies itself heuristically, as a source of insights, and the theories of Tynyanov amount to a program for a revealing type of literary historiography.

Until now, the theories of Tynyanov have not had much practical impact on the writing of literary histories. One reason is, perhaps, that they have not been widely known. Moreover, they could not be influential in this moment of revived historical contextualism. A third reason, however, is that they make the writing of literary history very difficult. Historical contextualism is an acceptable method of scholarship precisely because its necessary incompleteness can be acknowledged. Everyone knows that the whole context can never be known or represented, and most people assume, often incorrectly, that to exhibit just a piece of the context may be more illuminating than it is distorting. But according to the immanent theory of Tynyanov, to abstract some elements from a total structure or system, and to ignore the specific function of these elements within the system, are typical errors of traditional literary history. The very concept of tradition, for example, "proves to be the unjustified abstraction of one or more of the literary elements of a given system . . . and the consolidating of these with exactly the same elements of another system, in which they possess a different 'emploi,' to form a supposedly unified, apparently unbroken series."[52] In other words, Tynyanov puts so much emphasis on structure, on the correlation and interaction of parts within a system that, in contrast to contextual explanations, he could not think it useful to perceive only an area of the system. Following

[51] Tynyanov and Jakobson, "Problems in the Study of Literature and Language" 80. In "On Literary Evolution," published a year earlier, Tynyanov had maintained that "the concept of a steadily evolving synchronic system is a contradiction" 449.

[52] Tynyanov, "On Literary Evolution" 437.

his prescriptions, literary historians would have to compare system with system.

Thus Tynyanov's theory would impose an extraordinary amount of reading and reflection. One notes that Bloom's immanent theory, which is much simpler to carry into practice, has been used as a basis for literary histories, for example, the one by Sandra Gilbert and Susan Gubar. It requires only that we compare a text with a few previous texts. Presumably the type of literary history envisioned by Tynyanov will be created gradually by many persons over a period of time.

Of course, such a literary history, if it is ever produced, will not be a complete explanation. Tynyanov does not utterly deny the value of "research into the psychology of the author and the building of a causal bridge from the milieu, from the life of the author outside literature and from his class position to his works" (457). But as the reductive phrasing leads one to expect, he advances a Medusa's head of arguments to diminish the importance of such considerations. Nevertheless, they remain important, even in Tynyanov's final formulations, and any sophisticated literary history must now draw on both immanent and contextual considerations.

8

The Functions of Literary History

IN HIS GREAT ESSAY *ON THE ADVANTAGE AND DIS-advantage of History for Life*, Nietzsche criticizes our modern surfeit of historical knowledge. What distinguishes the present age from all past ones, he says, is that we know so much more about them than they did about each other. This knowledge is unhealthy. "Alien and disconnected" images from many times and places, a "carnival of gods, customs, and arts" fill our minds as a spectacle, but none are felt to be ours. As they collide in our minds, they are all relativized, and so also are whatever convictions and values characterize the present moment in history. Existence can be truly vital only within a closed horizon, argues Nietzsche; without this, a person, a people, and an age are threatened with "the dangerous disposition of irony with regard to itself, and from this the still more dangerous one of cynicism."[1] I of course am the type of historical critic Nietzsche scorns. I have encountered this same analysis of the modern mind repeatedly in essays by Paul Bourget, Hugo von Hofmannsthal, and many others from the turn of the century, in T. S. Eliot's "The Waste Land" and derivative poems and novels since, and in the latest accounts of postmodern culture. I do not believe it. In me, as Nietzsche

---

[1] Friedrich Nietzsche, *On the Advantage and Disadvantage of History for Life*, trans. Peter Preuss (Indianapolis: Hackett, 1980) 28, 10.

would have predicted, the only effect of his argument is to provoke criticism of it, and this chapter is inspired by Nietzsche because it is conceived against him.

As a relativizing historian, I see of course that Nietzsche's antitheses and hierarchy of values—his contrasts of belief and irony, life and knowledge, the closed horizon and the carnival of ideas, with the exalting of the former—are cliches of romantic cultural nostalgia. Few persons, if given a choice, would actually prefer to live within a closed horizon. I note the irony and paradox with which Nietzsche himself speaks of those who live "unhistorically," that is, without knowledge of history. They are, he says, like rosy-cheeked Alpine rustics, "a pleasure to behold"; or like the herd of cattle peacefully grazing; or, descending further the biological scale, like trees contented with their roots (11, 8, 20). Furthermore, as Nietzsche points out, it is only historical knowledge—his study of ancient Greece—that gives him a vantage point outside the historicist culture he attacks, enabling him to see it and criticize it. Thus Nietzsche is, as always, himself the man he criticizes, the ironical and historical consciousness.

Yet Nietzsche has asked the right question—what is the advantage and disadvantage of history for life?—and in this he is admirable, for many theorists refuse to face the issues he raises. Paul Veyne, for example, maintains that the study of history is an intellectual pleasure "identical with mere curiosity." Its goal is "knowing for the sake of knowing," and it has no effects on the way one feels or lives. Outside the library, says Veyne, a historian eats, votes, and "professes sound doctrines" just like other people.[2] We might similarly argue that the questions literary history addresses are of great interest in themselves—the problem of literary change, why? and how?; the problem of context, of the impact on literature of political and social realities. To pursue such questions, we need no justifica-

---

[2] Paul Veyne, *Writing History: Essay on Epistemology*, trans. Mina Moore-Rinvolucri (Middletown: Wesleyan UP, 1984) 64.

tion. It is enough to say that, having intellects, we are curious. Or we might argue that literary history seeks a systematic understanding of relations. It explores the similarities, influences, threads of filiation, and the like, that link authors and texts, and thus it structures the past. The understanding of works that literary history achieves is a disciplinary one and has at least a formal claim to being an objective understanding. In our modern world, understanding must be disciplinary and systematic if it is to be persuasive. Yet these points concern the function of literary history as knowledge only. Nietzsche scorns the "pure thinkers who" are "satisfied with mere knowledge, whose only goal is the increase of knowledge" (23). He probes the impact of this knowledge on feeling and action, and I shall try to emulate him with respect to knowledge of literary history.

The function of literary history cannot be quite the same as that of history, whatever the latter's function may be. There is, to be sure, a kind of literary history that is indistinguishable from history or historical sociology, and it fulfills the same functions. Veyne describes it very well as a "history of literary life and taste": "Who read, who wrote? What was read and what was the conception of literature and writers? What were the rituals, the roles, and the roads taken by literary life? What writers, great or lesser, created fashions, were imitated?" (67). Most literary histories include information of this kind, but it is not their chief concern. If it were, they would not much interest literary readers.

Literary history differs from history because the works it considers are felt to have a value quite different from and often far transcending their significance as a part of history. In other words, literary history is also literary criticism. Its aim is not merely to reconstruct and understand the past, for it has a further end, which is to illuminate literary works. It seeks to explain how and why a work acquired its form and themes and, thus, to help readers orient themselves. It subserves the appreciation of literature. The function of literary history lies partly in its impact on reading. We write literary history because we want to explain, understand, and enjoy literary works.

Thus, while the necessities of historical explanation select what texts are included in the narratives of literary history, so also do other criteria that may broadly and vaguely be termed aesthetic. Because it is so deeply penetrated and determined by critical aims and evaluations, literary history seems to many historians a loose, compromised type of history, and one of the earliest literary historians, Georg Gervinus, who had first been trained as a historian, declared that evaluations had no place in this type of discourse. He was almost the last literary historian to make this claim, and Gervinus's history is as thoroughly shaped by unstated critical evaluations as are all others.

Before developing his attack on the consciousness saturated with history, Nietzsche notes three positive uses of history for life that have obvious correlatives in literary history. The first chapter of this book mentions what Nietzsche calls *critical* history. Trampling all pieties under foot, this "puts the knife" to some portion of the past, judges, and annihilates it. "It is an attempt," Nietzsche shrewdly remarks, "*a posteriori* to give oneself a past from which one would like to be descended in opposition to the past from which one is descended" (22). Such literary history serves the needs of writers in the present, and examples of it are legion. We can cite T. S. Eliot's essays that praise poets of the seventeenth century while scoffing at Shelley, Byron, Tennyson, and the romantic tradition generally.

Nietzsche's *monumental* history corresponds to the type of literary history that concentrates on the greatest of past writers and seeks inspiration from them. Its approach to literature might be called humanist, since it hopes to support not only writers in their art but readers in living. For example, in his famous sonnet "To a Friend," Matthew Arnold praises Sophocles, who "saw life steadily, and saw it whole," and the speaker hopes, through reading Sophocles "in these bad days," to be infused with his "even-balanced soul." When literary history is written with this attitude, it assumes, in Nietzsche's words, that "the great moments . . . of humanity are linked throughout millennia," that "what is highest in such a moment of the distant past" is "still alive, bright and great," and can be made our own (15). Friedrich Schlegel's 1812 lectures on poetry might be cited as an example. Monumental literary histories that dwell only on the greatest works are rare, but passages of monumental criticism are common. In these passages, the historian urges that literary and human greatness "was at least *possible* once," as Nietzsche says, "and may well again be possible," and the reader "goes his way more courageously" (16).

This book has not considered critical or monumental literary history, for neither type pursues or values the aim of most literary histories, which is to offer a plausible version of past events. Both are deliberately "unjust" to the past, as Nietzsche puts it. Critical literary history deliberately rejects a historical point of view. It does not perceive the literature of the past in relation to the time and place that produced it, but selects, interprets, and evaluates this literature only from the standpoint of the present and its needs.

Because monumental literary history concentrates only on the greatest authors and texts, the past itself, says Nietzsche, "suffers *damage:* very great portions of the past are forgotten and despised, and flow away like a grey uninterrupted flood, and only single embellished facts stand out as islands" (17). Even the islands, moreover, are myths. "As long as the soul of historiography is found in the great incentives a powerful man receives from it, as long as the past must be described as something worthy of imitation . . . so long, at least, is the past in danger of being somewhat distorted, of being reinterpreted according to aesthetic criteria and so brought closer to fiction"

(17). In other words, monumental history must ignore aspects of the past that would render a writer or work less inspirational. I am not thinking only of the retouching of the past, as when we brush over class feelings, anti-Semitism, patriarchal attitudes, and so on, but of the subtler distortion that comes in making the past enough like the present for its example to be relevant. "How much that is different must be overlooked," Nietzsche points out, "how ruthlessly must the individuality of the past be forced into a general form and have all its sharp edges broken" if monumental history is to have its powerful effect (16)!

A function of many literary histories has been to support feelings of community and identity. In his sonnet that begins "It is not to be thought of that the Flood," Wordsworth writes,

> We must be free or die, who speak the tongue
> That Shakespeare spake; the faith and morals hold
> Which Milton held.

In other words, Wordsworth believes that there is a tradition and a canon of English literature, and that they help to create the language, religion, morality, and politics of England in his time. If Shakespeare and Milton still speak to us, the reason is that they have been factors in forming our contemporary civilization and hence ourselves. We identify with them and, hence, with each other, for we feel that Shakespeare and Milton are mutually ours. If we no longer responded to Shakespeare and Milton, Wordsworth says, we would not be the same people; our identity would have changed.

Wordsworth's view of tradition and its function is shared by many literary historians, and it is explicitly set forth and defended by Hans-Georg Gadamer in *Truth and Method*. It applies, mutatis mutandis, not only to national traditions but to those that form the consciousness of any social group. In this view, a history of literature, whether it be the literature of a nation, class, region, race, or gender, would help instruct us who we are individually and as a community. It displays the tradition in which we stand whether we will or no, for this tradition has formed us.

In fact, however, literary histories deal in a rather different way with tradition. When Wilhelm Scherer, for example, describes the *Minnesinger*, he intends that his contemporary German readers should identify with these medieval poets as German, but as he foregrounds certain qualities in these poets and ignores others, he is defining Germanness in a certain way. In other words, he reshapes the tradition in accordance with his own values; he specifies German identity as he would like it to be; and he hopes that, in doing so, he will have an effect in modifying the character of Germans. Traditions and identities exist, and literary historians try to discern them, but essentially they are ideas in dispute, and as literary historians describe them, they seek to remake the present.

I stress that histories of the literatures of regions, social classes, women, ethnic groups, and so on have the same functions as the national literary histories of the nineteenth century. They assert that the group in question has a literary tradition and that the works in it are valuable. Thus, in the strife of cultural politics, they confer cultural importance on the social group. They create a sense of continuity between past members of the group and present ones and, by describing a shared past, reinforce the sense of community in the present. They define the identity of the group in a certain way in opposition to other definitions of this contested concept. To members of the group, this definition has extreme importance, since it affects the way a person views himself and is viewed by others.

This literary history that traces a tradition corresponds in some ways to the type of history Nietzsche calls piously *antiquarian*. The antiquarian historian looks back "with loyalty and love" to the portion of the past from which he derives. But in doing so he distorts the past, for he is interested only in what lies within his own tradition and greets even its mediocre achievements with enthusiasm. "The antiquarian . . . has an extremely limited field of vision; by far the most is not seen at all, and the little that is seen is seen too closely . . . [he] cannot apply a standard and therefore takes . . . each individual thing to be too important" (19–20).

Critical, monumental, and antiquarian literary histories fulfill their functions by misrepresenting the past. If it is true, as I have argued, that literary history cannot depict the past as it actually was, objective representation cannot possibly be its function. Hence we might swing to the other extreme, and maintain that the function of literary history is to produce useful fictions about the past. More exactly, it projects the present into the past and should do so; it makes the past reflect our concerns and support our intentions. Here, certainly, we identify processes that take place in all literary histories. Yet such misrepresentations, valuable and necessary though they may be, are not the most important function. To claim otherwise would seriously misstate the aims of most literary historians. What is worse, it would grossly simplify the actual effects of literary history.

Most literary historians strive—impossibly—for an objective understanding of the past and would modify their critical, monumental, or antiquarian assertions if they perceive a conflict between these and what they believe is actually the case. The question we must ask is, what would be the function of a reliable literary history if it could be written? I have already indicated the usual answer: historical knowledge helps us to better understand, appreciate, or enjoy what we read. It reveals the background that makes the work meaningful and the aesthetic that makes it beautiful. Literary histories explain allusions in texts, establish the expectations associated with a genre in a given time and place, show how a work broke through a general crisis in aesthetic construction, demonstrate that it served or subverted a dominant ideology, and so forth.

This answer is correct, obvious, and states important functions of literary history. But it is also somewhat superficial and must be considered more deeply. For one cannot know just enough literary history to yield the helpful gloss. To orient a text toward the time and place that produced it alters our reading of it radically. Imagine, for example, the difference between medieval responses to the poems of Virgil and those of modern classical philologists. Works we read unhistorically speak to us directly or not at all. We do not take them as characteristic of a time and place, but as true or false, beautiful or ugly, moving or irrelevant. In other words, the medieval reader interpreted Virgil within his own frame of reference, for he had no idea that there was any other frame of reference. As a result, he made Virgil's texts address his own concerns, find him immediately, speak thoughts and feelings he could share. In youth we are all naive, unhistorical readers. At age fourteen we do not place and explain a sonnet as the expression of courtly love conventions; it is a moving utterance of an emotion we identify with. Fitzgerald's *Rubaiyat* expresses not the skeptical hedonism that was typical of late Victorian poets but the melancholy truths of life. As adults we are still more or less unhistorical when we read works from cultures or from pasts about which we know little.[3]

When a text is placed in literary history, seen as

---

[3] See Hans-Georg Gadamer, *Truth and Method* (New York: Crossroad, 1989) 270: "The text that is understood historically is forced to abandon its claim that it is uttering something true. We think we understand when we see the past from a historical standpoint, i.e. place ourselves in the historical situation and seek to reconstruct the historical horizon. In fact, however, we have given up the claim to find, in the past, any truth valid and intelligible for ourselves. This acknowledgement of the otherness of the other, which makes him the object of objective knowledge, involves the fundamental suspension of his claim to truth."

belonging to the past, and especially to a past about which we are informed, it becomes at once a part of a world that is not our own. It locates itself at a distance from ourselves and is viewed as the expression of an alien mentality. This, to emphasize, is our immediate orientation. It may change if we find that the text does after all speak directly to us as if from our own world. But our first expectation, created by modern historiography, is that the lived experience uttering itself in the text will be very different from ours.

Moreover, a literary history views a work as part of a group of works, within a narrative that may contain many works and systems of them. Often the many works discussed are radically diverse, yet in most cases the literary historian views them more or less impartially. For these reasons, literary history tends to prevent us from strongly identifying with any single work. It forms responses that are relativized and somewhat detached. "To take everything objectively," says Nietzsche ironically, "not to be angered by anything, to love nothing, to comprehend everything, how gentle and pliable this makes one!" (48).

To many readers it will seem that if this is true, literary history comes at a very high cost. But would they prefer the closed horizon Nietzsche feigns to endorse? If literary history tends to prevent us, in some degree, from completely committing ourselves to any work, it compensates by activating in us a dialogue with the past. Thus a literary work becomes a more complicated experience, aesthetically and intellectually, even if it also becomes a less immediately relevant one. And there are many works—whole periods—that we could not and would not read without the mediation of literary history. Thus, to learn to read with the perspective of literary history is like growing up. We encounter a wider, more diverse world of books, expressing mentalities that challenge us by their difference.

A text from the past embodies a lived experience, an

aesthetic, a culture that is alien. Of course, it is not completely alien. Continuities and universals in human experience are the themes of antiquarian literary history and humanist criticism. But most literary histories emphasize the difference of the past. Taine writing as a Frenchman on English literature, Nietzsche on the birth of tragedy in ancient Greece, Benjamin on the German *Trauerspiel* of the seventeenth century, Greenblatt on the English Renaissance are—it goes without saying—misrepresenting the past and reading their own mentality into it, but they are also studying a time, place, and culture that they assume to be very unlike their own. They are trying to perceive, understand, and explain it as accurately as they can. As literary historians they undergo, and make us experience with them, the shock to values, the effort of imagination, the crisis for understanding and sympathy of every profound encounter with the past that seeks to be objective. Here, incidentally, is why literary history cannot surrender the ideal of objective knowledge of the past. Though the ideal cannot be achieved, we must pursue it, for without it the otherness of the past would entirely deliquesce in endless subjective and ideological reappropriations. A function of literary history is, then, to set the literature of the past at a distance, to make its otherness felt.

Some readers will object that the past, if thus represented, becomes merely an aesthetic spectacle. It entertains, perhaps it expands imagination, but literary history, so conceived, could have no impact on the present or the future. To meet this objection we must recall the opening of Nietzsche's essay. A purpose of teaching in the humanities, it is usually said, is to keep the past alive, to make it a part of present consciousness. If we ask why this is desirable, one answer is that we do not want to be prisoners of the present.

The cultural diversity of the past can be viewed as a set of options, a reminder of alternatives and possibilities. A literary historian is usually a specialist in some past age. In imagination he inhabits that other time and place as well as his own. He sympathizes with its values and ideals. Often this state of mind is described pejoratively as escapist, and indeed, many a specialist has no effect on the present except to disturb the dust of a library. But the specialist is a citizen of two ages and, thus, can bring one to bear critically on the other.

Nietzsche makes this point when he says that his training as a classical philologist puts him into an "untimely" relation to the present. His statement can be generalized as a function of literary history. "Only so far as I am the nursling of more ancient times, especially the Greek," he says, "could I come to have such untimely experiences about myself as a child of the present age." For "I do not know what meaning classical philology would have for our age if not to have an untimely effect within it, that is, to act against the age and so have an effect on the age to the advantage, it is to be hoped, of a coming age" (8).

INDEX

Designed by Bruce Gore.

Composed by A. W. Bennett, Inc.,
in Trump text and display.

Printed on 50-lb. Glatfelter, B-16,
and bound in Holliston Roxite
by Edwards Brothers, Inc.